LOVING GOD WITH
ALL YOU'VE GOT

LOVING
GOD
WITH ALL
YOU'VE GOT

Reordering Your Life's
Priorities and Perspectives

SUNDER KRISHNAN

WingSpread Publishers
Camp Hill, Pennsylvania

WingSpread Publishers
3825 Hartzdale Drive · Camp Hill, PA 17011
www.wingspreadpublishers.com

A division of Zur Ltd.

CONTENTS

PREFACE

When we think of someone who really loved God, it is hard to find a more passionate soul than the poet Frederick Faber. Look at what poured out of his heart through his quill:

> I love thee so I know not how
>   My transports to control;
> Thy love is like a burning fire,
>   Within my very soul.
>
> For thou to me art all in all,
>   My honor and my wealth,
> My heart's desire, my body's strength,
>   My soul's eternal health.
>
> Burn, burn, O love, within my heart,
>   Burn fiercely night and day,
> Till all the dross of earthly loves
>   Is burned, and burned away.
>
> O light in darkness, joy in grief,
>   O heaven begun on earth;
> Jesus, my love, my treasure, who
>   Can tell what Thou art worth?
>
> What limit is there to this love?
>   Thy flight, where wilt Thou stay?
> On, on! Our Lord is sweeter far
>   Today than yesterday.
>
> O Jesus, Lord, with me abide;
>   I rest in Thee, whate'er betide;
> Thy gracious smile is my reward;
>   I love, I love Thee, Lord.[1]

While not able, perhaps, to write poetry like Faber, you may have no trouble joining him in such lyrical affirmations of your love for God. You feel what you sing; your heart is almost effortlessly involved in any interaction with God, be it in private or corporate worship.

You feel deeply, too, for people. Your heart goes out to them in their need, and you gladly do what you can to meet that need. And what you cannot meet, you wish you could. God has gifted you with the spiritual gifts of mercy and a fertile imagination that allows you to grasp the great realities of God and humanity intuitively, almost automatically invoking your feelings. In addition, you score high as a "flexible feeler" on the Myers-Briggs Temperament Indicator (MBTI); people are never an interruption in your schedule. (I have been happily married to someone like this for over thirty-one years.)

If so, you may find the contents of this book almost totally superfluous—though I sincerely hope that you will still read it and that some parts of it might contribute to the ongoing enlarging of your soul and the renewing of your mind.

I, on the other hand, have the spiritual gifts of teaching, knowledge and leadership. I score very high as an introverted, highly structured thinker on the MBTI—not exactly a combination most prone to make a person very loving. If obeying the commandment to love God is to reach the lofty heights of mystics like Faber, I am discouraged from even taking the first step; the destination seems unreachable.

As for loving people, I am not naturally drawn toward the hurting, the outcast and the underdog. I am not adept at counseling, and I find it a tremendous emotional drain. I will never love people the way my wife does.

Despite all that, I can't opt out of obedience to Jesus' commandment to love God and my neighbor as myself. So I have had to think long and hard about loving God and people. How do I find a balance between (on the one hand) imposing unachievable demands on myself, given who God has made me, and (on the other hand) rationalizing halfhearted obedience or even neglect of the two commandments that Jesus said encapsulate the whole law of God?

Some insights have helped along the way. I think it was C.S. Lewis who defined love as doing something for the lasting good of another. And Scott Peck expanded this idea when he suggested that we might think of love as the deliberate stretching of ourselves for the growth of another human (be it spiritual, emotional, physical or intellectual). That certainly helped me, for I could readily see how I could use the unique blend of my gifts and temperament to spur this kind of growth in others. I have done so for over thirty years (and joyfully, most of the time).

But when it comes to loving God, things get more complicated, at least for a thinker like me. Even a moment's reflection is sufficient to show us that neither Lewis' nor Peck's definition of love can apply to God. In his book *The Four Loves*, Lewis clarifies the distinction among four kinds of love. Two that pertain to our current discussion are *eros* and *agape*.

You may have learned that *eros* refers to erotic or sexual love; it certainly includes that, but it embraces much more. Lewis defines it as *that love in which the object of the love is also the source of the love*. So when I say that I love my wife because she is gentle and compassionate, that is *eros* love. I love her because of something that is already in her. She, the object of my love, is also the source of my love.

Agape, on the other hand, is not like that at all. When a faithful husband nurses an incapacitated wife through a long illness lasting several years, it is not primarily what she is or has that calls forth his loving service but largely something that she needs. His love is a completing love, giving her what she does not have. In this case, she, the object of his love, is not the source of his love. If the husband is a Christian, the source of his love is God.

When we are called to love people, it is a call to both *eros* and *agape* love—to love them for who they are but also to love by giving, completing. But God is perfect; He needs nothing and never will. We cannot complete Him by giving Him what He lacks. In that sense, the usual Christian call to love God with *agape* love is meaningless. (Many a sermon on Jesus' thrice-repeated question, "Simon, do you love me?" has made much of the fact that the third time Jesus asks the question, He uses *agape*, suggesting that we should love God with *agape* love. That is impossible given the meaning of *agape*.)

Thus I have come to the conclusion that the only way I can love God is with *eros* love; *He, the object of my love, must also be, and increasingly become, the source of that love*. I love Him because *He is*, revealed in many cases by what *He does*—in me, for me and through me. I can love Him only as He keeps revealing His loveliness to me. So I sing Faber's hymns not as affirmations of what is true of me but as expressions of what I long for. I latch on to powerful contemporary songs like "Pure and Holy Passion,"[2] "Holy Love, Flow in Me,"[3] "Lord, Reign in Me"[4] and others.

In one sense, therefore, every chapter in this book is, at its most fundamental level, intended to bring readers into God's presence and give specific contours to the outpouring of their hearts, a longing for a fresh revelation of His beauty and majesty, so that they may indeed love Him more and stretch themselves deliberately for the lasting good of others in ways that are consistent with their unique dispositions, gifts and temperaments.

When it comes to the specific content of this book, I am reminded of a poster I once saw on the wall of an educational institution, attributing these words to Isaac Newton: "If I can see further, it is because I have stood on the shoulders of giants." I do not claim to see further than anyone, but whatever helpful insights the chapters of this book possess are because of giants whose shoulders I have stood on. I will mention four whose influences are evident in this book:

I am indebted to **Os Guinness** for his insights into the shaping and molding power of modernity and the subversive infiltration of culture into the tenets and practice of our faith.

Eugene Peterson's wide shoulders have contributed immeasurably to the development of what I call an "appropriate stance" in doing ministry—namely, that *ministry is not my gift to God but God's gift to me. It is not what I do but what Christ is doing all around me and inviting me to join in.*

John Piper has made the fruit of Jonathan Edwards' massive spirit and intellect accessible to me. He has taught me that *God's glory is both the goal and fuel of all ministry* and that *the appropriate and sufficient motivation for all obedience is "future grace" and not discipline or self-denial.*

C.S. Lewis, a giant in anyone's estimation, has helped me understand and explain *the complexities of Christian doctrine in layman's language.*

If this book does nothing more than get you to read some of the works of these authors, and other giants, whom I have quoted liberally, I will deem the effort more than worthwhile. I gladly dedicate this book to the giants who have lent me their shoulders.

I want to thank Doug Wicks for taking the initiative to turn a sermon series into a book, and Dave Fessenden, for his painstaking editing of the transcribed tapes, chasing after permissions for quotations, etc.

I am delighted to express my gratitude once again to the congregation of Rexdale Alliance Church, who are the first ones to listen to my messages, including the ones that led to this book. Their feedback, encouragement and striving to obey what they hear God saying serve to improve the messages for the subsequent listeners and, in this case, readers.

When it comes to loving God and people, my wife of thirty-one years continues to be my role model and silent mentor. As for our children, their spouses and our three grandchildren, even I don't need a book and a lifetime of reflection to love them. They make it so easy.

Sunder Krishnan
Toronto, Canada
March 2003

Notes

1. Frederick W. Faber, "O Jesus, Jesus," *Hymns of the Christian Life* (Camp Hill, PA: Christian Publications, 1978), 41.
2. Mark Altrogge, "Pure and Holy Passion," People of Destiny International, 1988.
3. Andy Park, "Holy Love, Flow in Me," Mercy/Vineyard Publishing, 1995.
4. Brenton Brown, "Lord, Reign in Me," Vineyard Songs (UK/Erie), 1998.

1. The Anatomy of Idolatry

I've been a Christian now for about forty years, and for thirty-nine of them God has given me the privilege of studying and teaching His Word. And as happens in every other aspect of life, the learning curve was at its deepest early on. Almost every day, every week, I would be learning something new from the Word of God about my life with Him. And even after the curve flattened out, as it necessarily must, I can still remember many occasions—though sometimes separated by months or even years—when some absolutely new perspective on God and His nature would enrich my understanding and filter into my life as well.

This happened to me several years ago while I was reading the passage from Mark 12 in which a teacher of the law asks, "Of all the commandments, which is the most important?" (12:28). The words that were imprinted on my mind and wouldn't let go of me were Jesus' answer:

> "The most important one," answered Jesus, "is this: 'Hear, O Israel, the Lord our God, the Lord is one. Love the Lord your God with all your heart and with all your soul and with all your mind and with all your strength.' The second is this: 'Love your neighbor as yourself.' There is no commandment greater than these." (12:29-31)

Jesus said elsewhere that "all the Law and the Prophets hang on these two commandments" (Matthew 22:40). In

1

other words, these commandments are not only primary; they actually capture all of God's written revelation—hundreds of pages in the Bible. And the obvious question is this: If Jesus Christ is who He says He is, and He has seen fit to hang the entire revelation of God upon two commandments, doesn't it behoove us to give serious attention to those two commandments?

The words Jesus used to answer the question are from Deuteronomy 6:4-5. Known as the *Shema*, this passage was one of Israel's standard prayers. They had recited it over and over until it had lost its meaning; familiarity had dulled their perception.

So it is for us. How many times have we heard "Love the Lord your God with all your heart and with all your soul and with all your mind and with all your strength" and "Love your neighbor as yourself"? We have heard it so often that familiarity has dulled our perception. But if Jesus places the weight of the entire revelation of Scripture upon those two commandments, we must allow their full weight to penetrate us deeper than ever before.

What does it mean to love God with all of our hearts? The word *heart* is a very significant Bible term, occurring hundreds of times. And it is used almost equally to represent four things: our personalities (who we are), our minds, our will and our feelings. It is a comprehensive word in the Bible, used to describe the very core of our beings as it expresses itself in what we think, what we choose and what we feel.

Proverbs 4:23 says, "Above all else, guard your heart, for it is the wellspring of life." The heart is the source out of which everything flows. God asks us to love Him with the source of our whole being, feeling, willing and acting. Where does one start on such a comprehensive journey?

Since Jesus began with a quotation from Deuteronomy, it is not surprising that we find the answer in Deuteronomy as well:

> If a prophet, or one who foretells by dreams, appears among you and announces to you a miraculous sign or wonder, and if the sign or wonder of which he has spoken takes place, and he says, "Let us follow other gods" (gods you have not known) "and let us worship them," you must not listen to the words of that prophet or dreamer. The LORD your God is testing you to find out whether you love him with all your heart and with all your soul. (Deuteronomy 13:1-3)

God Himself has given us a test—the number one test—of whether we love God with all of our hearts: It is the extent to which we have followed other gods. We are speaking, of course, about idolatry, an issue that is mentioned over 200 times in the Bible.

When I think of idolatry, one question comes immediately to my mind: Why does a God who is absolutely awesome and sovereign get so worked up about hunks of wood and stone covered with gold and silver? Have you ever thought of that? The reason is that idolatry is the most comprehensive description of the sinful imagination of our hearts. It is the most basic shape in which sin comes in this world.

Such a concept, of course, is hardly original with me. In the first chapter of *No God But God: Breaking with the Idols of Our Age*, Os Guinness and John Seel discuss the theological problem of idolatry with great insight and relevance.[1] In the remainder of this chapter, I want to summarize their argument in a simpler form and show how it applies to our theme of loving God with all our hearts. I freely admit that I will be following their train of thought quite closely (and at times directly quoting them), because to tinker with their argument for the sake of novelty would be to significantly reduce its effectiveness. (As Thomas Oden once observed, theologians—and, I may add, expositors of God's Word—are called not to novelty but to faithfulness to the truth.) With this caveat, let's plunge ahead.

How Idols Are Made

Guinness and Seel note that "the ultimate idol factory is the human heart."[2] And so it is critically important for us to understand the manufacturing process and the nature of the product that rolls off the assembly line.

Let's begin at the beginning. In Genesis 1 and 2, God made human beings in His image and asked them to exercise that divine image in two directions. They were to exercise dominion over creation and to do it in total dependence upon God. Dominion and dependence were the two primary expressions of the divine image in Adam and Eve, with absolutely no tension between these two functions. Total dependence upon God was in perfect harmony with absolute control over creation. On the one hand, He was a transcendent God. He was totally other. The gap between the creature and the Creator was infinite, and that transcendent God gave them meaning and significance as they depended on Him. On the other hand, He was the immanent God. He walked with them in the cool of the day. And the immanence of God gave them power and authority and control.

Enter the serpent in Genesis 3 and, with him, sin. Sin changed dominion over creation to the domination of creation—including domination of one another. It turned dependence on God to independence of God and dependence instead upon the creation for meaning. What was in perfect harmony before is now in tension, because these expressions of God's image were twisted.

This tension between the desire for control (domination of creation) and the desire for meaning (dependence on creation) is seen, for example, in something as simple as a new opportunity at work or a new challenge in a sport. First we think, *I can do that.* That's domination. But then another thought occurs to us: *But what if I fail?* That's dependence. Dependence and domination begin to fight with one another.

This is why idols are always created in our hearts in pairs. We are made to worship, and even when we push God out of the picture, we still need gods—something we can worship. And so we create gods in pairs. We create a nearby idol that is small enough that we still remain in control (domination). And then we create a faraway idol that is big enough to give meaning (dependence) but is never close enough to threaten our control.

This pairing of gods goes all the way back to the Canaanite pantheon from which Israel got so much of its idolatry. Baal, who is mentioned in the Bible, was their nearby god and gave them power, magic, strength and control; but they had another god in their pantheon that was the overarching, big-picture god that gave them meaning, and they never brought the two together.

How do these things work out in our lives today? We don't have Baals and gods of silver and stone, but we have nearby and faraway idols—and they always come in pairs. Let's start with the most common ones: power, possessions and popularity, and the money that is necessary to buy most of those things. This is a group of nearby idols that confers a lot of control. If we have power, possessions, popularity and a lot of money, we have a lot of control over things, circumstances and people. But that doesn't give meaning by itself, so we need a faraway idol.

One faraway idol is some kind of delusion of immunity or invincibility: "I can't be beaten; no one can stop me." It may even go so far as to become an illusion of immortality. I once read in the newspaper about a seminar that promised to make you twelve years younger, and I'm sure thousands of people signed up for it.

This desire for faraway idols is one reason why many people who are totally committed to power, possessions and popularity love to talk "philosophy." They'll talk about meaning and significance, worshiping the faraway god that goes along with them.

A specific example of this is New Age philosophy. The nearby idol is the power of the human mind, positive thinking, Silva mind control, Gerhard seminars, psycho-cybernetics, etc. And the goal in every case is power—power in business and personal relationships, power over problems, etc. The faraway god, of course, is pantheism—borrowing shamelessly from Eastern mysticism, which speaks of the individual as a god.

Another form that is very popular in our society is the nearby idol of expertise linked to the faraway idol of progress. We live in a society that needs an expert for everything. And we believe, so many of us do, that if we can become the best at whatever, that's going to give us a degree of control— a salary increase or a new job. The faraway idol is a philosophical assumption, somewhere along the line, that we are improving humanity in this whole process.

Richard Keyes shared how music works in this way:

> A musician friend once described to me the worldview of many of his colleagues. They had a nearby idol in the highly disciplined skill of playing their instruments (to which they would offer almost anything in sacrifice), and had the faraway idol in the belief that the arts were inherently, morally uplifting and ennobling to the human race.[3]

Then there are idols of the body. The nearby idols are diet and fitness. "If I can be thin enough, shapely enough, strong enough, look attractive enough, I'll be in control of my life." That's the way most diet and fitness plans are sold today, isn't it? The faraway idol is self-esteem. "If I can get and keep myself in shape, I'm going to feel so good about myself that nobody is going to stop me. I can conquer the world."

And let's not forget religious idols. The nearby idol is legalism. Change life into a bunch of rules and regulations where every question has pat answers, and that gives you a tremendous amount of control over yourself, because you don't have to think. And when you don't have to think, nothing ruffles your calmness and your established way of thinking. Not only that, but it gives you tremendous control over others. One of the major motivating forces behind legalism is the extent of power it confers over other people. The Pharisees, of course, were classic examples of this.

What is the faraway idol of legalism? It is the heavily edited version of Jehovah of the Old Testament. The Pharisees forgot about justice, truth, righteousness and mercy, while they majored on giving tithes of mint and anise and cumin. And Jesus confronted them on this distortion. They edited their mission too. Their mission was not to worship Jehovah but to travel over land and sea to get people to believe their rules and regulations. And Jesus confronted them on that in Matthew 23.

One reason legalism is so hard to break is that anything that conveys control and meaning together is unbelievably powerful. The nearby idol is small enough that you can retain control. The faraway idol is big enough to give you meaning, but because it's far away it won't affect the way you live.

What about Christians? We believe in God the Father, the Son and the Holy Spirit, the Apostles' Creed and all the rest. We don't make idols in our hearts, do we? No—what we do is just split God into two. We create a nearby version of the God and Father of our Lord Jesus Christ who is a heavily modified version of the God of the Bible, obtained by rejecting those parts of the Bible that don't fit into our picture of God. Not interested in missions? Then forget about everything the Bible says about God and missions. Not interested in living the simple lifestyle? Then forget what the Bible says about money. Not interested in justice? Forget everything in the Bible about justice.

The resulting nearby idol does not challenge the control area of our lives. How about the faraway idol? He is also Yahweh, and we accept everything that the Bible says about Him. We maintain God's revelation intact, but we never approach Him in worship. That way He stays far away, and the nearby god by which we actually live is never challenged. Keyes summed it up beautifully: We create the nearby idol by miniaturizing God. We create the faraway idol by vaporizing God.[4] Miniaturization and vaporization are the means by which we commit idolatry.

The Biblical Basis

This idea of the dual nature of idolatry, based on original sin, hangs together very well, but is there any explicitly biblical warrant for understanding the Fall in this way? It rings true to life, but is there a biblical basis as well? Well, there is. Let me begin with Jeremiah 23:23: " 'Am I only a God nearby,' / declares the LORD, / 'and not a God far away?' "

Jeremiah used the same terminology we've been using to understand idolatry. One main theme of Jeremiah is false prophets. These false prophets were busy borrowing visions, dreams and eloquent sayings from one another, then preaching them as God's truth. And God responds, "I have heard what the prophets say who prophesy lies in my name. They say, 'I had a dream! I had a dream!' How long will this continue in the hearts of these lying prophets, who prophesy the delusions of their own minds?" (Jeremiah 23:25-26).

The delusion that they were preaching was that God would continue to bless Israel, that they would not go into captivity in Babylon (see 27:14). And God's answer to that delusion was to shatter their idolatry. Their nearby idols were power, control and influence over the people; their faraway idol was an edited version of God that focused on all the blessings of the covenant and forgot its responsibilities.

God said to them, "Am I only a God nearby . . . and not a God far away?" (23:23). In other words, He was saying, "You think I'm just somebody you can modify, put into your pocket and take out when you need help? I am the same God

THE ANATOMY OF IDOLATRY

far away who is nearby, the transcendent God who gives you meaning. You can't push Me away. You can't draw Me close to yourself by changing Me. I'm unchangeable, nonnegotiable, un-relocate-able."

And when God says that His Word is "like fire . . . and like a hammer that breaks a rock in pieces" (Jeremiah 23:29), He says that in contrast to the false prophets' dreams and prophecies that soothe people and say, "'Peace, peace' . . . when there is no peace" (6:14; 8:11) and don't ruffle their idols at all.

That's the Old Testament. What about the New Testament? In Acts 17, again set in the context of idolatry, Paul visited Athens for the first time. And in this city that was given over to idols, Paul was "greatly distressed" (17:16). The Greek word translated "distressed" is akin to the English word *paroxysm*. Paul's heart was deeply moved when he saw the city given over to idols, a pantheon of gods and goddesses.

Most of them were nearby gods, but they had an altar to "the unknown god." That was their faraway god. The near ones let them control their own lives, but this "unknown god" gave them some meaning.

Notice what Paul does in his message: He systematically strips the faraway idols and the nearby idols. And he does it alternately. "Now what you worship as something unknown I am going to proclaim to you" (17:23). He took the faraway God that was "out there" and brought Him in all of His awesome power right next door to the Athenians.

Paul continued by emphasizing what this God is really like—what they had edited out (in ignorance). "The God who made the world and everything in it is the Lord of heaven and earth and does not live in temples built by hands" (17:24). He's not a nearby god. He can't be assimilated into your pantheon of idols. He is far away.

Then he says, "He is not far from each one of us. 'For in him we live and move and have our being' " (17:27-28). This

God that Paul is proclaiming is so close that we actually live in Him. He's surrounding us. He's everywhere—above us, underneath us, all around us, inside us, outside us.

But Paul goes back again to take another slap at the nearby god. "Therefore since we are God's offspring, we should not think that the divine being is like gold or silver or stone" (Acts 17:29).

Twice he dismisses the faraway gods. Twice he dismisses the nearby gods. And then he declares, "He himself gives all men life. . . . He made every nation of men . . . he determined the times set for them and the exact places where they should live . . . so that men would seek him and perhaps reach out for him" (17:25-27). Same message, isn't it? You cannot split the transcendence of God from the immanence of God. You can't make an idol out of the immanent God and put the transcendent God out there in the distance. It cannot be done.

That's why Paul ends his message to the Athenians with a call and a warning: "For he has set a day when he will judge the world with justice by the man he has appointed. He has given proof of this to all men by raising him from the dead" (17:31).

Now as soon as we mention judgment, we get concerned. It seems to paint an ignoble picture of God, doesn't it? It makes Him sound like a modern-day political despot who ruthlessly eliminates anyone who refuses to submit to His authority. If you don't worship Me, says God, then I'm going to judge you.

But that line of thinking is all wrong. As Paul says, "The Lord of heaven and earth . . . is not served by human hands" (17:24-25). Our God doesn't need our worship. Our worship doesn't make Him any more glorious. And our rebellion doesn't make Him any less glorious. Therefore, if God threatens us with judgment for idolatry, it's because something else is at stake—something we stand to lose and wouldn't want to lose if only we realized it.

Dangers of Idolatry

Why does God warn against idols? There are two reasons. First, idols are lies, and they deceive us. The nearby idol promises you control, and the faraway idol promises meaning, but the nearby idol ends up controlling you, and the faraway idol deserts you in the crisis of life. The very idols that you create to increase your control over creation end up enslaving you. Power, possessions, popularity, positive thinking, expertise, diet, fitness, legalism—all of them become masters that control you. It's the very nature of idols to deceive. And in the crises of life (including the biggest crisis of life—death), the faraway idols disintegrate into nothing. No meaning is possible. It is to save us from this double danger of slavery under the guise of freedom and meaninglessness under the guise of meaning that God warns us to repent of our idolatry.

The second reason for God's warning against idols is the recurring principle in the Bible that those who worship idols become like them. We become like what we worship. The Psalms, Israel's worship manual, emphasize this repeatedly and bluntly:

> The idols of the nations are silver and gold,
>   made by the hands of men.
> They have mouths, but cannot speak,
>   eyes, but they cannot see;
> they have ears, but cannot hear,
>   nor is there breath in their mouths.
>   (135:15-17)

That last line, "nor is there breath in their mouths," is the one that got my attention. Breath in the Bible is always a sign of life. One result of the idols in our hearts is that we become a "breathless" people, not able to communicate life-giving words to others. We cannot see reality, hear reality, smell reality or taste reality, so we cannot communicate reality to people.

It is to save us from this that God says, "Repent of your idols." And He roots this warning of judgment in the resurrection of Jesus Christ: "He has given proof of this to all men by raising him from the dead" (Acts 17:31).

True Worship

In Jesus we find incontrovertible evidence that the transcendence and immanence of God cannot be divided. "For in him dwelleth all the fulness of the Godhead bodily" (Colossians 2:9, KJV). You couldn't have more of God than was in Jesus. But "the Word became flesh and made his dwelling among us" (John 1:14) and touched us and ate with us and drank with us. Transcendence becomes immanence without any diluting of the transcendence.

That's why all true worship of God is characterized by both love and fear. That's why Frederick Faber can write:

> Oh, how I fear Thee, living God,
>   With deepest, tenderest fears,
> And worship Thee with trembling hope
>   And penitential tears!

And yet he can also say in the same hymn:

> Yet I may love Thee, too, O Lord,
>   Almighty as Thou art,
> For Thou hast stooped to ask of me
>   The love of my poor heart.
>
> No earthly father loves like Thee,
>   No mother, e'er so mild,
> Bears and forbears as Thou hast done
>   with me, Thy sinful child.
>
> Father of Jesus, love's reward,
>   What rapture will it be,
> Prostrate before Thy throne to lie,
>   And gaze and gaze on Thee![5]

We tremble and we love. That's genuine worship. With idolatry, we can focus only on fear of the faraway idol and love of the nearby one. But the two are blended inseparably in the worship of the true God.

And this is the good news. If those who worship idols become like them, what happens to those who worship Jesus? We become like Him! That's what Second Corinthians 3:18 says, isn't it? "And we, who with unveiled faces all reflect the Lord's glory, are being transformed into his likeness with ever-increasing glory, which comes from the Lord, who is the Spirit."

Guinness observes:

> The imagination of our sinful hearts has such a reality creating power that the nonexistent is invested with its own dynamic. Thus, regardless of what the mind "knows," the imagination of the heart can change the mind. It can turn lies into truth, fictions into reality, no-gods into gods and the quite incredible into the utterly credible. This idol-making propensity of the imagination of our hearts is a continuing and deadly threat to faith.[6]

And then he finishes with this observation on moral theism:

> To say that there is one God and no god but God, is not the conclusion of a syllogism nor simply an article in a creed. It is an overpowering, brain-hammering, heart-stopping truth that is a command to love the only one worthy of our entire and unswerving allegiance.[7]

This "unswerving allegiance" to God must be a daily, even moment-by-moment, decision. "Having once turned from idols to the living God, our task of keeping on turning is never done," Guinness says.[8]

You alone know how you have fragmented God. You alone know what nearby idols you have manufactured to give you control and how you have pushed away the God of the Scriptures, editing Him into a faraway god who gives meaning but is not close enough to change our lives.

It is time to repent of this sin. It is time to bridge this artificial separation. It is time to let the faraway God of the Scriptures be the nearby God, to once again yield control of our lives to Him, to live in dependence on Him and thus draw our significance from Him by cooperating with Him to advance His kingdom in and through us.

Notes

1. Os Guinness and John Seel, eds., *No God But God: Breaking with the Idols of Our Age* (Chicago: Moody, 1992).
2. Ibid., p. 27.
3. Ibid., p. 42.
4. Ibid., p. 47.
5. Frederick William Faber, "My God, How Wonderful Thou Art," *Hymns of the Christian Life* (Camp Hill, PA: Christian Publications, Inc., 1978), 17.
6. Guinness and Seel, p. 24.
7. Ibid., p. 206.
8. Ibid., pp. 24-5.

2.
Loving God's Word

To love God with all our hearts, as we saw in the last chapter, means dealing with the issue of idolatry. This can be done only by bringing the faraway God nearby so that He can be the same God close up that He is far away and can root out all competing idols.

But how do we do it? How do we bring this faraway God nearby? The passage in Deuteronomy that Jesus called the greatest commandment—"Love the LORD your God with all your heart and with all your soul and with all your strength"—contains the clue to this puzzle in the very next verse: "These commandments that I give you today are to be upon your hearts" (6:5-6). To love God with all our hearts inevitably means to love His commandments or His law with all our hearts as well.

This emphasis on having a heart for God's commands is not unique to the book of Deuteronomy. It is echoed later on in the history of Israel, when the prophets began to talk about the new covenant. The Lord declares through the prophet Jeremiah, "I will put my law in their minds / and write it on their hearts" (Jeremiah 31:33). And then in the New Testament, Paul proclaims the new covenant, saying, "And hope does not disappoint us, because God has poured out his love into our hearts by the Holy Spirit" (Romans 5:5). The love of God and the law of God are upon our hearts.

One of the essential marks of a regenerated heart is that it has impressed on it both the love of God and the law of God. Speaking to His disciples in the Upper Room, Jesus said, "Whoever has my commands and obeys them, he is the one who loves me" (John 14:21). So to love Jesus is to love the law of God, just as to love God the Father is to love the law of God. The love for God's law and the love for God are inseparable.

Our initial reaction to such a close linking of law and love may be like a teenager's reaction to a parent's rules—it seems restrictive. It cramps our style. We don't like the image of a Father telling us what to do and what not to do. We resent control. We cry, "Legalism!" We may even quote Scripture, such as John 1:17, which says, "For the law was given through Moses; grace and truth came through Jesus Christ." We then conclude (erroneously) that grace and truth are opposed to law.

We also make a division between the Old Testament and the New Testament, between the God of the old and the God of the new. The God of the Old Testament is angry, wrathful and vengeful, but the God of the New Testament is loving and warm and gentle. We make distinctions between an unapproachable God and a loving, gentle Jesus Christ who died for us.

All these distinctions seem to have some credibility, but they are based on one massive omission. When we look in the Psalms, Israel's worship manual, it is immediately obvious that there is a serious flaw in our instinctive pitting of law against love and grace. In the Psalms, the whole focus is on the relationship between the people of Israel and their God. This relationship, as expressed in their worship and prayers, embraces the full gamut of human emotion laid bare to its roots—whether joy, bitterness or sorrow. What amazes me, though, is that pulsating through the entire book is an attitude to the law of the Lord that is totally different from our customary reaction to God's law and our inbuilt tendency to oppose it to love and grace.

The very first psalm includes this verse: "But his delight is in the law of the LORD, / and on his law he meditates day and night" (1:2). Remember, when the psalmists referred to "the law of the LORD," they probably meant either Deuteronomy or the Pentateuch (the first five books of the Bible, from Genesis through Deuteronomy).

Then there is Psalm 119, that magnificent tribute to the law of the Lord. Fourteen times law is linked to what is in a person's heart. Typical of this group is verse 111: "Your statutes are my heritage forever; / they are the joy of my heart." Twenty-two times the law of the Lord is linked to love and delight and joy. Consider verse 97: "Oh, how I love your law! / I meditate on it all day long." R.C. Sproul, in one of his sermons on the Old Testament, asked the penetrating question, "How long has it been since you heard a Christian say, 'Oh, how I love Your law, O God'?"[1]

The psalmists considered the law of the Lord not a restriction but an incredible privilege, one that set them apart from every other nation in the world:

> He has revealed his word to Jacob,
>   his laws and decrees to Israel.
> He has done this for no other nation;
>   they do not know his laws.
> Praise the LORD.
>   (147:19-20)

How different is their attitude toward the law of the Lord than ours! Somewhere along the line, we have missed the boat in our understanding of the law of the Lord. What is it that the psalmists got hold of that made them respond with such joy to the law of the Lord, while we think that it cramps our style and makes life restrictive rather than joyful?

The clearest answer is found in Psalm 19. The first six verses speak of God's glory as revealed in the heavens. The psalmist is looking at the night sky and sees in it a demon-

stration of the might and majesty of God. And we sense
something of the psalmist's emotion every time we read of
some new discovery in astronomy. I marvel at the mind of
God that can conceive and create such massive objects, then
fling them out over incomprehensible distances of space—
and yet with such incredible order and precision that a space-
ship such as *Voyager II* can travel 2 billion miles in twelve
years and arrive at its destination only four minutes late!
Don't you marvel at the order of God?

But after that, in the next five verses, the psalmist talks
about—you guessed it—the law of the Lord. And once again
we see his inescapable delight in that law:

> The law of the LORD is perfect,
>   reviving the soul.
> The statutes of the LORD are trustworthy,
>   making wise the simple.
> The precepts of the LORD are right,
>   giving joy to the heart.
> The commands of the LORD are radiant,
>   giving light to the eyes.
> The fear of the LORD is pure,
>   enduring forever.
> The ordinances of the LORD are sure
>   and altogether righteous.
> They are more precious than gold,
>   than much pure gold;
> they are sweeter than honey,
>   than honey from the comb.
> By them is your servant warned;
>   in keeping them there is great reward.
>   (19:7-11)

Where does this joy come from? C.S. Lewis calls it the joy
"of a man ravished by moral beauty."[2] Just as he looks at the
physical world and is ravished by the physical order in the
universe and what it implies about the mind that created it,

so he looks at the law of the Lord and he sees moral order there and is ravished by the beauty of that moral order.

He also exults in what that order will do in his inner world. He says that the law of the Lord can revive the soul, make foolish people wise, bring joy to the heart and give light to the eyes. Just as God has so beautifully ordered outer space, so too, through His law, He can order the "inner space" within our lives, and that's what the psalmist rejoices in.

In Psalm 119, a much longer version of the rhapsody of Psalm 19, we find several more ways that the inner world is ordered by the word of the Lord. It makes for purity (9-11), stability (165), authority (46), liberty (32, 45) and maturity (98-100). No wonder the psalmists are so excited about the law of the Lord!

But mixed in with this love for the law we find another emotion: fear, or awe. The law is rooted in the holiness of God and is able to bring about this wonderful transformation in our lives because it is holy. And so the psalmist also fears. For example, in Psalm 19:11 he says, "By them [these statutes that revive the soul, make wise the simple, etc.] is your servant warned."

Remember how the writer of Psalm 19 began with a meditation on the heavens? Just before he gets to a discussion about the law, he talks about the sun. He says, "It rises at one end of the heavens / and makes its circuit to the other; / nothing is hidden from its heat" (19:6). When the psalmist speaks of the heat of the sun, he's not talking about 70-degree weather; he's talking about 100- or 115-degree heat. I grew up in that kind of heat, and I know what it's like. It penetrates every nook and cranny inside the house; even in the shade you sweat, and the air is like the blast of heat when you open an oven door.

The psalmist is saying that the law of the Lord is like that. The law of the Lord penetrates every nook and cranny of my life and reveals my flaws; this is a necessary precursor to the wonderful things that the law does in my life as well. And so the psalmist cries out, "Who can discern his errors? / Forgive my hidden faults" (19:12). Who can discern my errors? I can't, but the law can. The law brings out my hidden faults. And he asks for victory over temptation: "Keep your servant also from willful sins; / may they not rule over me. / Then will I be blameless, / innocent of great transgression" (19:13). The psalmist fears the law of the Lord—but at the same time he loves it.

Psalm 119 gives us the exact same kind of balance between love and fear, often set in close proximity. Verse 113 says, "I love your law"; verse 120 says, "I stand in awe of your laws." Verse 161 says, "My heart trembles at your word"; verse 163 says, "I love your law."

One morning as I was meditating on this juxtaposition of fear and love, I prayed, "Lord, how do these two things go together?" And suddenly it struck me: The only law that I can love in this way is the law that is holy enough to make me tremble. Because the law is holy, rooted in the unchanging character of God, it means that I can't fiddle around with it. I can't manipulate it, twist it or assimilate it to suit myself.

More important, because this law is unchanging and unchangeable, because it cannot be assimilated or manipulated, I have hope that it can affect and change me. I have hope that it can do everything the psalmists say it can do: restore my soul, make me wise, give joy to my heart, enlighten my eyes and bring purity, stability, authority, liberty and maturity into my life. And so I can say, "I fear Your law, O God, because I don't like this kind of penetration, but I love Your law with all my heart. It's the only thing that can change me—and I want that kind of change in me."

That's why the psalmist prays, "Keep me from deceitful ways; / be gracious to me through your law" (119:29). We think of grace as the opposite of law; we always pit these two things in tension. But the psalmist says, "Be gracious to me— but *through* your law." It is always by grace, but it is grace through His unchanging law. "What God has joined together, let man not separate" (Matthew 19:6) is true not only of marriage but also of law and grace.

Now that we understand how loving God with all our hearts also means loving the law of the Lord with all our hearts, the practical question is this: How do we recapture this love for the law? How do we unlearn all these wrong notions that we have about law? How do we get to the point where we can say, "I love your law, O God—even as I fear it"?

Distorting the Word

This unlearning begins with the realization that we have a distorted view of God's Word, along with an underlying disrespect for language. A.W. Tozer notes that this can lead to terrible self-deception:

> Mankind appears to have a positive genius for twisting truth until it ceases to be truth and becomes downright falsehood. By overemphasizing in one place and underemphasizing in another the whole pattern of truth may be so altered that a completely false view results without our being aware of it.[3]

And Charles Colson, in one of his magnificent essays in his book *Who Speaks for God?* tells us how this twisting works in practice:

> In a culture infected with moral AIDS, words lose all meaning; or, they are manipulated to obscure meaning. Thus taxes become "revenue assessment enhancements"; perversion is "gay"; murder of unborn children is "freedom of choice"; Marxism in the church is called "liberation theology." These are all good words (in the Nazi era, "the final solution" had a nice ring to it also). And everyone just nods unquestioningly.[4]

Colson concludes with this ominous statement: "But when words lose their meaning, it is nearly impossible for the word of God to be received."[5] We live in an age when words have lost their meaning. And so the first thing we have to do if we are going to learn to love the Lord our God with all our hearts, and to love the law as well, is to begin to recapture the original meaning of the language of the Bible. We've got to learn again a new vocabulary—without redefining it, psychologizing it or socializing it.

We need to read the Word of God. We cannot love what we've never read even once from cover to cover. We need to read it and keep reading it until we are willing to understand and use words like *heaven, hell, sin, salvation, saved, lost, rebellion, independence, submission, authority* and *freedom.* I encourage you to start reading and keep reading the Word of God until you learn a whole new vocabulary—without redefining what God has said.

But that is not enough. It is necessary but not sufficient, because there is a second factor that has led to this distortion of our approach to the Word of God. We lack what A.W. Tozer calls a "sanctified imagination":

> The value of the cleansed imagination in the sphere of religion lies in its power to perceive in natural things shadows of things spiritual. It enables the reverent man to "See the world in a grain of sand, and eternity in an hour." The weakness of the Pharisee in days of old was his lack of imagination, or what amounted to the same thing, his refusal to let it enter the field of religion. He saw the text with its carefully guarded theological definition and he saw nothing beyond. . . . I long to see the imagination released from its prison and given to its proper place among the sons of the new creation. What I am trying to describe here is the sacred gift of seeing, the ability to peer beyond the veil and gaze with astonished wonder upon the beauties and mysteries of things holy and eternal. The stodgy pedestrian mind does no credit to Christianity.[6]

We have lost our imaginative abilities when it comes to God's Word. They have become book words, ink words, not words voiced by the Spirit of God. We have to learn to reengage our imaginations when reading the Word of God. How do we do that?

Visualizing, Personalizing, Vocalizing

I can only share with you what has been helpful to me in my own experience. I have begun to consciously and deliberately exercise my imagination as I read the Word of God so that I begin to visualize what is being said. Visualization helps me put myself in the place of the original hearers of the Word of God; thus the Word becomes personalized. And when I visualize and personalize it, then the written Word becomes a living Word, a vocalized Word that evokes a response from me.

This threefold strategy of visualizing, personalizing and vocalizing has helped me to recapture, at least to some measure, this understanding of the law as a living Word and enables me to say, most of the time, "Oh, how I love your law, O God." I could give you dozens of examples of how, regardless of my mood or frame of mind, this process has filled my mind with images that have made ink words into living words. But in the interest of time and clarity, I will content myself with one specific illustration from Psalm 147, a passage that God was particularly using in my heart at the time that the content of this chapter was preached in sermon form. In verses 15-17 we read these words:

> He sends his command to the earth;
>   his word runs swiftly.
> He spreads the snow like wool
>   and scatters the frost like ashes.
> He hurls down his hail like pebbles.
>   Who can withstand his icy blast?

When I think of snow, frost and hail, I would be hard put to find three words that better summarize everything I detest about Toronto. After living in that city for thirty-three years, I still hate the winters. And on those few rare days when I am spared hail, frost and snow, the ever-present "icy blast" takes over, an ill wind that penetrates my parka and turns even the slightest bit of exposed flesh into rubbery, unfeeling skin.

Only one thing sustains me: the knowledge that spring is eventually coming. God stirs up the warm breezes and the waters begin to flow once again. I always look forward to my first walk in the spring—even though it is so early in the season that I usually have soggy feet on the way back!

On one such occasion I remember watching big ice floes out on the Credit River, massive rocks of ice it would seem, but when I looked carefully, what did I see underneath the ice? Water. The warm breezes had already started blowing and were cutting huge crevices into what were massive blocks of ice. Some of those crevices ran right through, breaking the big masses into two, and I knew that within a few weeks all the ice would be gone.

God says that is what His Word is like. Psalm 147:18 says, "He sends his word and melts them; / he stirs up his breezes, and the waters flow." And these very images of winter, which I hate, and spring, which I love, bring freshness and vitality to my understanding of the Word of God. His Word is like the warm summer breezes that begin to melt the massive, cold blocks of ice that are slippery, hard and jagged. Eventually it will eat away at them until the frozen things become flowing and warm. That's visualizing.

How did I personalize it? I've been personalizing it for years in many different ways. But let me tell you one insight that God gave me that might be helpful. Earlier on in that same psalm, I read that "the LORD builds up Jerusalem. . . . He heals the brokenhearted / and binds up their wounds" (147:2-3). And in a moment it flashed into my mind that brokenhearted and wounded people (often because of the hurts caused them by others) can be like snow and ice, with a coldness that produces hard and jagged edges in their relationships. They can depress, drain or even hurt other people, so others may not find them attractive. Most of us avoid people like that in the hope that they will go away.

But this psalm says that there is something else we can do: We can dare to hope and believe that God will send forth His Word once again like the summer breezes. And that which is cold and hard and jagged will begin to melt, slowly and inexorably. As God's Word gouges out huge crevices from that which was cold, as He cuts through and breaks apart things that seemed impregnable, that which was frozen begins to flow once again.

And when that image got hold of my mind that morning, I spent a lot of time praying for people I know who, in one way or another, are brokenhearted or wounded. Faith wells up in your heart and you say, "Yes! Yes! God's Word can do that. Send forth Your Word, O God." That's vocalizing what you have visualized and personalized.

You may say you're not the imaginative type. I used to say that for years. I used to hide behind it and denigrate my ability until I was challenged by authors such as Eugene Peterson and Calvin Miller. They all basically said the same thing: If you're a preacher of the Word of God, you have to be a wordsmith; you are called to be a poet. I don't think I'll ever publish poetry, but I am doing things in my prayers and preaching that I wouldn't have dreamed of doing several years ago.

The poet William Stafford was once asked when he decided to become a poet. I love his answer:

> I've thought about that, and sort of reversed it. My question is, "When did other people give up the idea of being a poet?" You know, when we are kids we make up things, we write, and for me the puzzle is not that some people

are still writing, the real question is why did the other people stop?[7]

The real issue in learning to visualize, personalize and vocalize and to love the law of the Lord is not ability but attitude. The last book of the law, Deuteronomy, concludes with this very significant challenge:

> When Moses finished reciting all these words to all Israel, he said to them, "Take to heart all the words I have solemnly declared to you this day, so that you may command your children to obey carefully all the words of this law. They are not just idle words for you—they are your life. By them you will live long in the land you are crossing the Jordan to possess." (32:45-47)

Is the Word of God just idle words for you—a "trifle," as the Amplified Bible puts it—or is it your life? One way to find out is to think about this question: What if I were to tell you that from this moment on, you will never again be allowed to read the Word of God—ever? You will never hear it preached, never hear it explained, never hear it read. What would be your reaction? Would it be a colossal tragedy of unimaginable proportions, or would life go on pretty much the way it is?

How you answer that question tells you whether this Word of God is a trifle in your life or is your very life. And if it is a trifle, if you honestly answered, "Yes, I'm afraid most of life would go on pretty much the way it is," I think you need to repent.

As a very specific mark of your repentance, I suggest that you take one simple step of obedience: Choose one week that is suitable and resolve to read Psalm 119 every day that week. It takes about eighteen minutes to read it slowly and reflectively—I timed it. Anyone should be able to afford eighteen minutes a day. This psalm is unique in that it is about the law of the Lord, written by a man who passionately loves the law of the Lord, and it is a prayer of illumination concerning the law of the Lord. So as you read it prayerfully, as you read it reflectively, three unique things will happen:

1. You will be exposing yourself to the law to relearn some vocabulary.
2. You will be getting insight into the heart of a man who is passionate about the law of the Lord.
3. You will at the same time be crying out to God, "Open my eyes that I may see / wonderful things in your law" (119:18).

If you do this, and if you persevere and do nothing else, I believe and pray that the frozen Word will become a flowing Word, that those ice blocks in your life will begin to melt until one day you are able to say with the psalmist, "Oh, how I love your law! / I meditate on it all day long" (119:97). And then what you began with Psalm 119, you will be able to continue with the other psalms and then with all of God's Word.

Notes

1. R.C. Sproul, from "O, How I Love Your Law!" from sermon series God's Law and the Christian. Available from Ligonier Ministries, P.O. Box 547500, Orlando, FL 32854.
2. C.S. Lewis, excerpt from *Reflections on the Psalms*, copyright © 1958 by C.S. Lewis, renewed by Arthur Owen Barfield, 1986, reprinted by permission of Harcourt, Inc., p. 60.
3. A.W. Tozer, *The Root of the Righteous* (Camp Hill, PA: WingSpread Publishers, 1955, 1986), pp. 83-4.
4. Charles Colson, *Who Speaks for God?* (Wheaton, IL: Good News Publishers, 1985), p. 68.
5. Ibid.
6. A.W. Tozer, *Born after Midnight* (Camp Hill, PA: WingSpread Publishers, 1989), pp. 93-5.
7. From an interview with Cynthia Lofsness, published (as "Dreams to Have") in William Stafford, *Writing the Australian Crawl* (Ann Arbor: University of Michigan Press, 1978), pp. 85-113 (quote from p. 86).

3.
Worship

One of my most delightful memories is from the summer of 1984, when for five days I had the privilege of camping among the Swiss Alps in beautiful Interlaken. I will never forget my walks along the shores of lakes Thune and Brienz nor the breathtaking drives through those magnificent valleys.

On one morning drive, as I was particularly exulting in the beauties around me, I looked over my shoulder at my two kids (ages eleven and eight at the time) in the backseat, their heads buried in comic books. In response to my energetic exclamations, they briefly looked around, said, "Oh," then went right back to their comics. That really irritated me!

The question is, why? Why was my enjoyment of the beauty of the mountains not sufficient on its own without an equal response from everyone else in the car? The answer to that question, which I will get to shortly, relates directly to yet another aspect of what it means to love God with all our hearts.

To love Him with all our hearts means to worship Him for who He is. When John got a glimpse of heaven, which he recorded in the book of Revelation, he saw inside that open door a crowd worshiping God, saying, "You are worthy, our Lord and God, to receive glory and honor and power, for you created all things, and by your will they were created and have their being" (4:11). The Bible may not fully explain *why* God created us, but it makes it very clear that the most appropriate response of the creature to the Creator is that of ascribing worth, or worship.

Of course, sin entered the picture and distorted this fundamental purpose; in the Garden of Eden the focus was shifted from God to ourselves. We became worshipers of ourselves and of created things. The rest of the Bible is the story of redemption, of God's providing for human sin without compromising His holiness and restoring His glory to the position of prime importance in the human heart, thus restoring us to our initial function as worshipers.

For example, there is the Exodus, that great model of redemption in the Bible, when God led the Israelites out of slavery to Pharaoh. What did Moses say in his repeated encounters with Pharaoh? "Let my people go, so that they may worship me" (Exodus 7:16; 8:1; 9:1; 10:3). Then when He did deliver them, He brought them to Sinai and gave them the law of the Lord and then the elaborate instructions to build the temple, the place of worship.

In the book of Numbers God gave Israel their marching orders—literally. He told them how they should move, three tribes at each of the compass points. And what was at the center? The tabernacle. The worship life of the people was always to be central, whether they stood still or were moving.

By the time we get to Malachi, the last book of the Old Testament, many centuries have passed. Israel has been in and out of the Promised Land and back in again. The temple has been rebuilt and worship has been restored, but the people's hearts are no longer in it. It has become an empty ritual, shot through with complaint and skepticism. And so God says to them, through the prophet Malachi, "Shut the doors; cancel the worship service. Go home. Don't light useless fires upon my altar. I don't want this kind of worship" (see 1:10). Worship has always been central to God's purposes for His people.

When we get to the New Testament, we see Jesus talking with a Samaritan woman, probing her heart, drawing her into a love relationship with Him. And what does he say to her? "Yet a time is coming and has now come when the true worshipers will worship the Father in spirit and truth, for they are the kind of worshipers the Father seeks" (John 4:23). Not often in the Bible does it say that God is seeking something. But He is seeking worshipers.

Then we come to Ephesians 1, where in the first fourteen verses Paul seems to ransack the Greek language to try to explain the wonder of our salvation and the riches of the grace God has lavished upon us. Three times he says that our salvation is "to the praise of his glorious grace" or to "the praise of his glory" (1:6, 12, 14).

Finally, in the book of Revelation we get a picture of heaven and the end of the age, when the whole work of redemption is complete. What do we see in heaven? We see people from every nation, tribe, people and language ascribing worth and honor and glory to God the Father and God the Son (see 7:9-12).

From beginning to end, it is very clear that we were made to worship, that sin distorted this fundamental purpose and that the entire work of redemption was to restore our function as worshipers of God. George Mallone, in his book *Furnace of Renewal*, put it this way:

> Humans were created to worship. It is as much a part of our constitution as our longing for the eternal or our sense of justice. To deny this natural response or to assume its irrelevance is like submerging a balloon under water. It continually springs up. If we are forced to suspend our worship of God, it does not mean that we stop worshiping, only that we direct its focus toward ourselves or toward another created object rather than to the Creator.[1]

That is why failing to praise God is the first step toward idolatry. We have been made to worship, and when we encounter God, it should be our natural response. And now I can answer the question I posed earlier about my Swiss Alps experience: Why did it bother me that my children did not appreciate the beauty around them? At a baseball game, if my team is winning, I can get excited even if everyone else is rooting for the other team. (In fact, if the other fans are not enjoying the game, it only adds to my enjoyment!) But it doesn't work that way when it comes to the mountains in Switzerland; there is something in the nature of their grandeur and their majesty that tells me that the only appropriate, sane response is contemplation, admiration and eventual exclamation.

You see, if my children decide to read comic books at the foot of the Alps, it doesn't take away from the grandeur of the Alps; it is my children who are impoverished. That's the way it is with God. The majesty and holiness of God (and all His attributes, for that matter) remain undiminished when we refuse to worship Him. It is *we* who become impoverished in the process. Worship is the only appropriate response to God.

Of course, as soon as we begin to speak of worship as a response, we see that feelings are involved. Worship and feelings go hand in hand. Look at some of the feelings that we find associated with worship in the Scriptures:

- Habakkuk 2:20: "But the LORD is in his holy temple; / let all the earth be silent before him." Stunned silence is one kind of emotional response in worship.

- Psalm 5:7: "But I, by your great mercy, / will come into your house; / in reverence will I bow down / toward your holy temple." Reverence, which is a combination of fear and awe, is another appropriate worship response.

- Isaiah 6:5: " 'Woe to me!' I cried. 'I am ruined! For I am a man of unclean lips, and I live among a people of unclean lips, and my eyes have seen the King, the

LORD Almighty.' " Conviction, sorrow and repentance are appropriate feelings in worship.

- Psalm 27:4: "One thing I ask of the LORD, / this is what I seek: / that I may dwell in the house of the LORD / all the days of my life, / to gaze upon the beauty of the LORD / and to seek him in his temple." The feeling of longing is another appropriate response in worship.

Stunned silence, fear and awe, conviction, sorrow, a passionate longing for God—these are all appropriate feelings that characterize and accompany true worship. I want to focus on one in particular—the feeling of longing—and how it relates to learning to love God with all our hearts.

As I noted in the preface, the English language uses a single word—*love*—to translate four different Greek words. Two of them that are pertinent to our present study of worship are *eros* and *agape*. *Eros* is linked to the English word *erotic*, but the Greek word means much, much more than the sexual or romantic dimensions that we associate with *eros*. In his book *The Four Loves*, C.S. Lewis develops the idea that *eros* is the kind of love in which the source of the love is also the object. Something in the person or thing that you love is what draws you to that person: "I love you *because* you are beautiful, wise, kind, etc." It's a taking love, a receiving love.

Agape, on the other hand, is a love in which the source of the love is not the object of the love but something else. It's a completing love, a giving love. You love not because of something in the loved one; rather, you love by giving to the loved one something that is *lacking* in him. You complete him out of your own resources. God, of course, loves us with *agape* love. It is a completing love, a giving love. As John 3:16 says, "God so loved the world that he *gave* . . ." The highest form of human love is when we are called to love other people not for what we can get from them but by giving to them what they lack in order to complete them.

The danger is that we can unthinkingly carry that over to the understanding of our love for God and say, "The most noble kind of love for God is a giving love, not a taking love—*agape*, not *eros*." But stop and think about that for a minute. What does God lack that we can give Him? What is incomplete in God that we can provide? Nothing! It is impossible to love God with a completing love.

Only one kind of love is really appropriate when it comes to our loving God: *eros* love, the love that is ravished by His beauty, by who He is in all His completeness and splendor, by what He can give to us. It is a taking love at heart, not a giving love. The love that saturated the minds and hearts of the psalmists and so many of the saints of God in the Scriptures is at its heart a *longing*, stimulated by the majesty and beauty of God—who He is in Himself and what that means for the one longing for Him.

All of which leads us to one conclusion: Where feelings for God are dead, worship is dead. R.C. Sproul put it so well when he said, "If people find worship boring and irrelevant, it can only mean they have no sense of the presence of God in it. It is impossible to be bored in the presence of God if you know that He is there."

But this creates another problem: We all know from experience that feelings cannot be commanded as an end to something else. I don't stand before the Swiss Alps and say, "Now, what should I be feeling? I suppose *awe* would be the appropriate response. Well, to what end should I be feeling awe? I should feel awe so that I won't be an impoverished person and can learn to appreciate nature. All right, then—come on, feel awe!" We all know it doesn't work that way.

Grief doesn't work that way either. As John Piper illustrates, if you get a telephone call in the middle of the night announcing that some loved one has died suddenly in an accident, what do you do? You don't say, "Now, what's the appropriate response here? I know—it's grief. To what end should I feel grief? So that I won't be a psychological basket case five years down the road because I didn't shed tears now. So, oh, my soul, start grieving!" We don't do things like that.

Grief, awe, anger—all of these feelings are appropriate, almost involuntary responses to stimuli from outside of us. So it is with worship. Worship, at heart, is not something that we command. It is our appropriate response to the self-revelation of God. But therein lies the paradox, doesn't it? We are called to worship Him, and yet it is something that He has to do for us.

John Piper, in his book *Desiring God*, cites a great illustration of this point from the pen of Edward John Carnell, a great apologist from Princeton University in years gone by:

> The paradox can perhaps be illustrated by a painter who deliberately tries to become great. Unless he strives, he will never be an artist at all, let alone a great artist. But since he makes genius a deliberate goal of striving, he proves that he is not, and never will be, a genius. A master artist is great without trying to be great. His abilities unfold like the petals of a rose before the sun. Genius is a gift of God. It is a fruit, not a work.[2]

"So is worship," Piper concludes.[3] But of course, we also know that great artists became that way because they strove for greatness. We need to hold both sides of the paradox. Worship without feelings is dead, so emotions are very appropriate. And yet we can't manufacture them. That doesn't mean, however, that we give up and say, "Well, it's all up to God."

There are two errors we need to guard against. One is to say, "Well, I won't worship God until I can do so perfectly. After all, the perfect state of worship is unencumbered, spontaneous joy in response to the greatness of God, delighting in His many full splendors. Well, I won't worship until I get there." That's the first mistake to avoid. The second, which flows from the first, is to say, "Besides, I can't do anything, because it is God's initiative; there is nothing left for me to do to make it happen." That isn't true either.

It is only in heaven that all our worship, all our feelings, will be spontaneous, voluntary, appropriate responses to God's self-revelation. But I have found from my own experience that the prior, earthly step to that heavenly worship, the stage where often all we can do is simply *long for* that kind of experience, is not only acceptable but essential.

Piper uses a very simple analogy. Imagine, he says, that you are climbing a mountain, knowing that there is a beautiful mountain spring at the top waiting for you. You do a great honor to that mountain spring when, after you have drunk great drafts and satisfied your thirst, you say, "Ah-h-h-h." But you also honor it while you are struggling up that mountain, longing for that drink.[4]

The longing after God is itself worship. And that's the kind of worship we see most often in the Scriptures—a worship in which we preach to our own souls, in which we use the help of aids to worship. The question is, what can we do, if anything, to put ourselves in the place where God can work on our behalf to draw us into worship? What can help us express our longing for God?

Music in Our Hearts

Many aids to worship are available to us, but the one that Scripture points to more than any other is words set to music, especially singing. There are over 150 commands and commitments in the Bible to sing. A number of these are directly related to the issue of loving God with all our hearts. Let's take a look at a few of these:

> Sing, O Daughter of Zion;
>   shout aloud, O Israel!
> Be glad and rejoice with all your heart,

> O Daughter of Jerusalem!
>   (Zephaniah 3:14)

> The LORD is my strength and my shield;
>   my heart trusts in him, and I am helped.
> My heart leaps for joy
>   and I will give thanks to him in song.
>   (Psalm 28:7)

> My heart is stirred by a noble theme
>   as I recite my verses for the king;
>   my tongue is the pen of a skillful writer.
>   (Psalm 45:1)

> Speak to one another with psalms, hymns and spiritual
> songs. Sing and make music in your heart to the Lord.
> (Ephesians 5:19)

> Let the word of Christ dwell in you richly as you teach
> and admonish one another with all wisdom, and as you
> sing psalms, hymns and spiritual songs with gratitude in
> your hearts to God. (Colossians 3:16)

One of the evidences of God's manifest presence among His gathered people is that we sing. In Psalm 132:8-9 the psalmist pleads, "Arise, O LORD, and come to your resting place, / you and the ark of your might. / May your priests be clothed with righteousness; / may your saints sing for joy." In verses 14 and 16 of that same psalm, God answers that prayer: "This is my resting place for ever and ever; / here I will sit enthroned, for I have desired it. . . . I will clothe her priests with salvation, / and her saints will ever sing for joy."

According to Zephaniah 3:17, God Himself sings for joy over us! Shouldn't we also sing for joy over Him? A.W. Tozer puts it this way:

> God Almighty is in the midst of us! He will save and re-
> joice over us with joy! God is happy if nobody else is and
> He will rest in His love. "He will joy over thee with sing-

ing"—the eternal God is singing! That's why I want our
congregations to sing. I don't require that they sing on
pitch—just that they sing with joy and enthusiasm.

I don't mind if the piano is out of tune, or if one fellow
is singing a little step behind the next fellow—that doesn't
bother me. But the lack of warmth and enthusiasm makes
me question the experiential life of Christians. The Christian Church has God in it and wherever God is, God will
joy over His people with singing. The singing of the
Church reflects the great God singing among His people.[5]

An inevitable implication of this is that the person who
loves God with all his heart is a person who has learned to
sing. How do we do it? I realize that we're not all musical (I'll
discuss that objection shortly), but how do we learn to sing
the way that we have been exhorted to in Scripture? Psalm
45 is a good place to begin. Verse 1 reads, "My heart is
stirred by a noble theme / as I recite my verses for the king."

We normally associate "verses" with poetry. There is nothing like the power of poetry to hook our imaginations. Eugene Peterson says that poetry "is not the language of
objective explanation but the language of imagination" and
that poets are "not trying to get us to think more accurately
. . . but to get us to believe more recklessly."[6] Good poetry
breaks us out of the ruts that we usually think in and helps us
see truth from a new angle.

That's what poetry did to the psalmist who wrote, "My
heart is stirred by a noble theme / as I recite my verses." He
was a poet, and as he started reciting the verses, his imagination got hooked; he became immersed in the reality of God,
and his heart poured out an expression of longing after God.

I wish I had the luxury of space and time to illustrate for you
the dozens (literally) of hymns and spiritual songs (contemporary expressions of passionate devotion and longing for God)
that have helped me share this experience of the psalmist. I will
content myself with just one example. Though the song I have

chosen may not be your favorite, remember that the *principle* applies to everyone, and let your heart be "stirred by a noble theme" as I recite my verses to you.

One morning as I took some time to pray, my heart was stirred by anything but noble themes! There was a lot of agitation in my spirit that morning. I asked God, "Where do I start? I'm preaching on Sunday morning, and I'm empty. You're going to have to make it real in my own life all over again."

My mind gravitated to a hymn that I have sung many times. And so I simply began to sing the first verse:

> O Thou, in whose presence my soul takes delight,
>> On whom in affliction I call,
> My comfort by day and my song in the night,
>> My hope, my salvation, my all![7]

I only had to sing that first line a couple of times, and all the ignoble thoughts started frittering away as God began to stir up noble themes in my soul. "My hope, my salvation, my all"—He was my hope, not for just some time in the future but for the next hour that morning. He was going to meet me and stir my heart by a noble theme. Then I sang the second verse:

> Where dost Thou, dear Shepherd, resort with thy sheep,
>> To feed them in pastures of love?
> Say, why in the valley of death should I weep,
>> Or alone in this wilderness rove?[8]

I imagined myself as a sheep being led by the Shepherd down a ravine. He was going to feed me—not with grass but with His love. So why should I weep? I wasn't exactly crying, but I had to confess to some self-pity, self-justification and irritation. We all know those experiences!

It was amazing, as I began to sing the second verse, how these negative and unhelpful feelings disappeared. Why? Because my heart was now full of anticipation of what God was going to feed me within the next hour. Why should I weep when my Shepherd is going before me to take me into pastures of love? Nothing stirs the emotions like anticipation.

Then came the verse that is, to me, one of the most image-laden in all hymnody. Every phrase of it stirs my imagination:

> He looks! And the thousands of angels rejoice,
>   And myriads wait for His word;
> He speaks! And eternity, filled with His voice,
>   Re-echoes the praise of the Lord.[9]

A single look from Him makes the angels rejoice. Do you know any look that can do that for you—a single look that can unleash floods of joy in your heart? It may have happened the first time you fell in love or during your first glimpse of your child or grandchild. But the only time this happens with this kind of intensity is when Jesus looks at us.

And so on that morning I prayed, *Lord, will You lower the veil that separates me from You, enough so that You can look into my eyes—long enough to unleash a flood of joy like I've never known before?* You can't pray that way without beginning to feel, at least a little bit, that He really is looking at you like that right now.

The second line, "And myriads wait for His word," reminded me that His look not only unleashes a flood of joy, but it also silences the restlessness of our anticipation. The image that came to my mind was of a crowd of subjects in a royal court, bustling with anticipation and talking among themselves because the king is about to arrive to make a proclamation. And of course, as soon as the king strides into the court and sits on the throne, there is immediate silence. "Myriads wait for His word."

Does our King speak? You bet He does. "He speaks! And eternity, filled with His voice . . ." Think of the wealth contained in the images in just that phrase! We normally think of space being filled, but this is talking about time. Eternity is filled with His voice. When God speaks, His voice, though spoken thousands of years ago, is not a word that disappears into silence when the vibrations die out.

The words I speak are gone in a matter of seconds. My voice disappears into the silence once the vibrations of the air stop. But He speaks, and eternity fills with His voice. From eternity past to eternity future, down through the corridors of time, the voice of the Lord is reverberating and hasn't lost a single bit of its power to reach and impact my spiritual ears.

Even more amazing is what happens when we listen to this voice that fills eternity. The fourth line of the hymn reads, "Re-echoes the praise of the Lord." When His Word hits my ears, it reverberates through my whole being and calls forth His praises.

Mechanical engineers speak of two different kinds of vibrations. For example, a car with a worn-out suspension bounces up and down—it vibrates at a certain frequency. That's the *natural frequency* of the car. But when you take that clunker over an old country road, a different kind of vibration sets in. This time the vibration is determined not by natural frequencies but by the frequency of the potholes in the road. That's called *forced* (or *sympathetic*) *oscillations*.

That's the sort of thing I imagine happening when God speaks, when His voice fills eternity and reverberates through my whole being. It overrides all the natural frequencies of my own heart—irritation, anger, frustration, self-justification, jealousy, envy, clamoring for recognition, pride—you name it. Those are my natural inclinations, but He comes with that word that reverberates through space and time and makes my heart beat in sympathy with His heart.

It's not hard to imagine how that kind of imagery can unleash powerful, passionate and heartfelt prayers. And so I prayed for the rest of the morning, *God, I rejoice that just Your look unleashes joy in my heart. But don't stop with Your look. Speak that word that fills eternity and overcomes every natural inclination of my heart. Make my heart vibrate in tune with Yours.* After that prayer, the last verse became incredibly sweet to sing:

> Dear shepherd, I hear and will follow Thy call;
>   I know the sweet sound of Thy voice;
> Restore and defend me, for Thou art my all;
>   And in Thee I will ever rejoice.[10]

Augustine prayed, "Thy voice surpasses in abundance of delights. Give me what I love."[11] Fifteen centuries ago he prayed that, and it has been my prayer for twenty-two years. Once you've heard the voice of God speak in such a way that you know He has spoken, there is no treasure on earth that comes close to that experience.

This is just a humble attempt to describe what the psalmist was talking about when he said, "My heart is stirred by a noble theme / as I recite my verses for the king; / my tongue is the pen of a skillful writer" (45:1). *Lord, stir my heart as I recite my verses for You, O King! Make my tongue the pen of a skillful writer!*

Objections

When I advocate the devotional use of music, I often hear certain objections. Some say, "Well, I'm not into hymns." That's possible. In Ephesians 5:19 Paul talks about other kinds of music too: "Speak to one another with psalms, hymns and spiritual songs." Spiritual songs are the contemporary expressions of praise that are appropriate in every culture, for the Holy Spirit isn't confined to one generation or one century. In every age, He is moving the people of God to write their praises in vital expressions of joy.

It is perfectly appropriate to use contemporary songs devotionally, but it should not be at the expense of neglecting hymns. The command from God is: "Speak to one another with psalms, hymns and spiritual songs." Why? As one wise man observed, "Every now and then we need to let the hours be silent so the centuries can speak." These great hymns of the faith, which God has chosen to preserve for hundreds of years, show us how to let the hours be silent so the centuries can speak to us. Through their classic phrases, thoughts and concepts, our imaginations can be stirred in ways that we never knew were possible.

The hymn I quoted earlier, "O Thou, in Whose Presence," was written over 200 years ago. "A Mighty Fortress Is Our God" was written 500 years ago. When we sing those hymns, a time miracle takes place, because they reverberate with the voice of God that transcends the centuries. We can be transported to the side of Martin Luther when he stood on trial before his enemies. If you sing "A Mighty Fortress Is Our God" five or six times in a row, you will know how Luther felt when he wrote it. The hours become silent and the centuries begin to speak to us and pour their strength into our lives.

It's incredible presumption on our part to dismiss as irrelevant what God has chosen to preserve for centuries, don't you think? Humility, if nothing else, requires us to pay attention to the great hymns of the faith along with the contemporary music.

One thing I would encourage you to do is to make sure that the contemporary music you use devotionally is rooted in the truth of God. Colossians 3:16 says, "Let the word of Christ dwell in you richly as you teach and admonish one another with all wisdom, and as you sing psalms, hymns and spiritual songs with gratitude in your hearts to God." Worshiping God this way with all our hearts is very much a part of learning to love the law of the Lord and letting it dwell within us. An open Bible and an open hymnal work together as two of the most powerful tools for spiritual heart stimulation I've ever known.

A second objection is simply "But I'm not a musician." Well, that's true about me, and it's well known in my home.

In fact, the standing joke among my children when they were growing up was that I cannot carry a tune long enough—they claimed that I was off-key as soon as I started singing! The fact that the other three members of my family all sing very well doesn't help much either. But it certainly hasn't stopped me, because the Bible says that I should sing and make music in my heart to the Lord.

When God commands us to sing, it is not a test of our ability—it is a test of our love. Or, as Oswald Chambers said it much more beautifully, "The real issue is not whether you have a voice, but do you have a song?" The Scripture says, "He put a new song in my mouth, / a hymn of praise to our God" (Psalm 40:3).

Another objection may be voiced in this way: "Well, I agree with you that heavenly worship—that unencumbered joy in response to the majesty of God—is inaccessible. And you say that my desire for that experience, a longing for God, is appropriate earthly worship. But I'm not that far yet; I don't even identify with that. About all I can do is to lament the fact that I have no longing for God."

Simply lamenting a lack of desire may be a perfectly appropriate starting point in worship for some of us. The psalmist declared in Psalm 57:7, "My heart is steadfast, O God, / my heart is steadfast; / I will sing and make music." A basic act of the will is necessary in such a situation. You simply declare, "No, Lord, I don't even have the longing. That's how bankrupt my soul is. But, God, I want it. And so I choose to put myself in a place where Your divine initiatives can seize me. I choose to put myself in a place where you can stir my heart. I choose to read the verses so my imagination may be stirred by them."

If you don't own a hymnal, invest a few dollars and get one. As I said before, an open Bible and an open hymnal are two of the most powerful tools that I have found to help me learn to love God with all of my heart and to love His law as

well. If you don't know where to start, look at the index in
the back. Most hymnals have a topical index; look for hymns
that emphasize the majesty and greatness of God.

But maybe your attitude is "I'm not going to do it. I just
don't want to sing." Sometimes that's understandable. A
friend of mine told me that when he was very young, he was
taken by his father in front of a group of people and asked to
sing. Of course, he didn't want to sing (which is understandable—I'm an adult, and I wouldn't want to sing before an audience either!), and when he refused, he was taken away and
spanked severely. It's not hard to understand why someone
like that might have a problem with singing!

God doesn't ask us to sing to show us off before an audience. He doesn't ask us to sing so that He can get some glory
to fulfill some deficiency in Him. He asks us to sing so that
our hearts can be stirred by a noble theme, so that we can begin to love Him with all our hearts, so that we can become
that much richer in our souls. The cost of not singing is colossal. It is *we*, not God, who stand to lose if we refuse to sing.

Charles Darwin is known for his book *Origin of the Species*.
What he is far less known for is his very wise observation on
what happens if we insist on refusing to let our hearts be
stirred by music and poetry:

> Up to the age of thirty, or beyond it, poetry of many
> kinds . . . gave me great pleasure, and even as a schoolboy
> I took intense delight in Shakespeare, especially in the
> historical plays. I have also said that formerly pictures
> gave me considerable, and music very great delight. But
> now for many years I cannot endure to read a line of po-
> etry: I have tried to read Shakespeare, and found it so in-
> tolerably dull that it nauseated me. I have also almost
> lost my taste for pictures or music. . . . I retain some taste
> for fine scenery, but it does not cause me the exquisite
> delight which it formerly did. . . . My mind seems to have
> become a kind of machine for grinding general laws out

of large collections of facts, but why this should have
caused the atrophy of that part of the brain alone, on
which the higher tastes depend, I cannot conceive. . . .
The loss of these tastes is a loss of happiness, and may
possibly be injurious to the intellect, and more probably
to the moral character, by enfeebling the emotional part
of our nature.[12]

I guess the greatest motivation we have for learning to love
God with all our hearts through singing is that if we refuse to
start, someday we may not be able to start when we want to.

Notes

1. George Mallone, *Furnace of Renewal* (Downers Grove, IL: InterVarsity Press,
   1981), p. 44.
2. Edward John Carnell, *Christian Commitment* (New York: Macmillan, 1957), p. 213,
   as cited by John Piper, *Desiring God* (Sisters, OR: Multnomah, 1986), p. 299.
3. Piper, ibid.
4. Ibid., p. 86.
5. A.W. Tozer, *The Attributes of God*, vol. 2 (Camp Hill, PA: WingSpread Publishers,
   2001), p. 191.
6. Eugene Peterson, *Reversed Thunder: The Revelation of John and the Praying Imagination* (San Francisco: Harper & Row, 1988), pp. 5-6.
7. Joseph Swain, "O Thou, in Whose Presence," *Hymns of the Christian Life* (Camp
   Hill, PA: Christian Publications, 1978), 324.
8. Ibid., second stanza.
9. Ibid., fourth stanza.
10. Ibid., fifth stanza.
11. Augustine, *Confessions*, bk. 11, ch. 2 (various editions).
12. Charles Darwin, "Autobiography," in *Life and Letters of Charles Darwin*, ed. Francis
    Darwin (New York: D. Appleton, 1896 [New York: AMS Press, 1972]), pp. 81-2.

4. Forgotten Fundamentals of an Integrated Life

Reginald Bibby, in a groundbreaking book from the 1980s, *Fragmented Gods: The Poverty and Potential of Religion in Canada*, began a disturbing argument by describing his experience at a Billy Graham crusade: On a hot summer afternoon in July 1981, Dr. Graham climbed into the pulpit and began to speak to some 20,000 people in McMahon Stadium in Calgary. I was among them. Now graying and showing some of the wear of a lifetime of mass evangelism, Graham proceeded with vigor and conviction to stress one of his central themes: *If you want everlasting peace, lasting joy, lasting hope, then you need Jesus Christ.*

Bibby then contrasted this image with a number of examples of sincere believers who were struggling with the moral and ethical implications of living out their faith on a daily basis: a young woman tempted to return to her former "partying" days and thus unable to enjoy either lifestyle; a salesman unable to resolve the tension between selling houses to make a living and being completely honest about the houses he is selling; an elected official wrestling with the ethics of political expediency; and so on. Finally, Bibby concluded that these people might well take exception to Billy Graham's claim that Jesus brings peace.[1]

Bibby argues that Canadians (and undoubtedly Americans as well) are becoming not less religious but simply more selective about what fragments of religion they adopt, so as to

maintain the relatively smooth transition from one role in life
to another. They handle the moral and ethical tensions of daily
living by determining when to be governed by one's religious
faith and when to be governed by the status quo or the prevailing opinion. He calls that (and rightly so) a fragmented life.

The opposite of a fragmented life is an integrated life.
Bibby uses the word *commitment*, but I like the word *integrated*
better, because commitment doesn't mean what it used to
mean. It's easy for a person to say, "I am committed to
church," but that may only mean, "I show up every Sunday
morning," while the rest of that person's life bears no marks
of any commitment to the claims of Jesus Christ at all.

An integrated life is an essential aspect of loving God with
all our hearts. We can see this in Proverbs 4:23: "Above all
else, guard your heart, for it is the wellspring of life." In other
words, the heart is who we are at the very core of our being. It
is something that spills over and affects everything we do. If
we love God with all our hearts, that means the center of our
lives—the essence of who we are—is one. With an undivided
heart, life will naturally be much more integrated. On the
other hand, if we do not love God with all our hearts, this
wellspring of life is not unified but fragmented, and the life
that flows from that heart is also fragmented.

As with so many other aspects of the Christian walk, living
an integrated life is both God's work and our work. For example, in Ezekiel 11:19 God promises as part of the new covenant, "I will give them an undivided heart and put a new
spirit in them." Obviously an undivided heart, out of which
flows an integrated life, is a gift of God to us and a work of
God within us.

But what is our response to that? Psalm 86:11 says, "Teach
me your way, O LORD, / and I will walk in your truth; / give me
an undivided heart, / that I may fear your name." God has
done what only God can do to give us unified, undivided
hearts out of which will flow integrated lives. But there is a re-

sponse on our part: to engage cooperatively with this God, turning into actuality what He has built potentially into our lives; to increasingly make our lives integrated.

This naturally leads to another question: What does an integrated life look like? We noted above several examples of the fragmented life. But what does an integrated life look like? What flows out of a heart that is integrated, unified, undivided?

Years ago I read a book by Os Guinness, *No God But God: Breaking with the Idols of Our Age*, in which he very briefly refers to what he calls "the five forgotten fundamentals of the Christian life." It is unfortunate that the thrust of his book did not allow him to expand on these statements, because as I read them, I realized that I had come across what, to me at least, was probably the most concise, brilliant description of the integrated life. His first three fundamentals, especially, help to answer the question of what an integrated life looks like.

1. The kingdom of God is God's here-and-now rule that orders and reorders our life's priorities and perspectives.

2. Discipleship is a lifelong apprenticeship under Jesus that teaches us to live as He would live if He were us.

3. Calling is the compelling source of vision, discipline and accountability for every sphere of life.[2]

While I could not hope to match the lucidity and brilliance of Guinness had he chosen to amplify these points, I gladly make a stab at them.

1. The Kingdom

The kingdom of God is God's here-and-now rule that orders and reorders our life's priorities and perspectives. The key phrase here is the ordering and reordering of our priorities. Christianity isn't just a passport to heaven. Christians are called to relate to Jesus Christ as a servant to a master,[3] and one essential characteristic of that relationship is that the servant's life is not his own. The first step in an integrated life is to acknowledge Christ's absolute authority over our lives—authority to determine and reorder our priorities.

A popular school of counseling, the nondirective method, was pioneered many years ago by Carl Rogers. Therapists who follow this particular method do not believe in telling their clients what to do but in leading them to "discover the truth for themselves." Jesus Christ is a wonderful counselor, but in no way is He a nondirective counselor.

I am reminded of that magnificent passage in the book of Joshua, just after Joshua had assumed the leadership of Israel:

> Now when Joshua was near Jericho, he looked up and saw a man standing in front of him with a drawn sword in his hand. Joshua went up to him and asked, "Are you for us or for our enemies?"
>
> "Neither," he replied, "but as commander of the army of the LORD I have now come." Then Joshua fell facedown to the ground in reverence, and asked him, "What message does my Lord have for his servant?" (5:13-14)

As a wise saint in my church put it, Jesus doesn't take sides; He takes over.

I'm afraid this is an aspect of our relationship with Jesus that we don't think about very much. Some of our popular worship songs are not much help. One song I enjoy singing leaves me with misgivings over one line: "Your love is so free of demands."

Think about that for a minute. Is Jesus' love free of demands? Yes, if we are talking about our relationship with Him. He does not make any prior demands upon us in order to earn His love. Salvation is a free gift, given not in response to our obedience.

But does Jesus make any demands on those whom He has sovereignly saved? Of course He does. I think it was G. Campbell Morgan who said, "He loves us the way we are, but He loves us too much to leave us that way." He makes a lot of demands upon our lives. Before we sing a line like "Your love is so free of demands," we need to understand what we mean. He is, as I said, a wonderful counselor, but He's a very directive counselor, at that. Our response, therefore, should be like Joshua's: "What message do you have for me, Lord?"

If we acknowledge that Jesus Christ, as commander-in-chief, has the right to order our priorities, we also need to be willing to let Him probe our present priorities. And I don't know of any two things that indicate our priorities better than the ways we spend our time and our money. Our use of time and money often reflects what we believe is going to give us significance and security.

I find, however, that most of us are unwilling to let Jesus probe the ways we spend our time and money. We are afraid of discovering what priorities, what belief system, those choices actually reflect. I have sometimes asked people to keep track of their disposable time and see where it really goes—and it is amazing how much resistance I run into sometimes! But that's the kind of honest, specific self-examination it's going to take if we really want to let Jesus reorder our priorities.

But precisely because our hearts are, in Jeremiah's words, "deceitful above all things" (17:9), we need the help of the searchlight of the Holy Spirit. So as we probe, we also need to pray the prayer of the psalmist: "Search me, O God, and know my heart; / test me and know my anxious thoughts. / See if there is any offensive way in me, / and lead me in the way everlasting" (139:23-24). There is a beautiful hymn that expresses in a different way the same kind of prayer:

> With that deep hush subduing all
>   Our words and work that drown
> The tender whisper of Thy call;

As noiseless let Thy blessing fall
As fell Thy manna down.

Drop Thy still dews of quietness
    Till all our strivings cease;
Take from our souls the strain and stress,
    And let our ordered lives confess
The beauty of Thy peace.

Breathe through the heats of our desire
    Thy coolness and Thy balm;
Let sense be dumb, let flesh retire;
    Speak through the earthquake, wind and fire,
O still small voice of calm![4]

An integrated life begins with our acknowledging the king-dom of God—God's here-and-now rule that orders and reor-ders our lives' priorities. But it is not something that we can pull off by ourselves. Certainly, private introspection, private probing of our priorities, is important and necessary, but even when guided by the Spirit, it is not sufficient. And this takes us to the second criterion mentioned by Guinness.

2. Discipleship

Discipleship is a lifelong apprenticeship under Jesus that teaches us to live as He would live if He were us. I want to focus on three words: *lifelong, apprenticeship* and *Jesus.*

Let us start, appropriately, with *Jesus.* The goal of disciple-ship is to become like Jesus Christ. Why were we saved? The Bible tells us very clearly: "For those God foreknew he also pre-destined to be conformed to the likeness of his Son" (Romans 8:29). That's our goal—to become like Jesus Christ.

And where can we find out what Jesus Christ is like? In the Gospels. In the twenty-two years that I have been privileged to occupy the pulpit of Rexdale Alliance Church, I have had many opportunities to study and preach through the Gospels, attempting to follow the advice of theologian Merrill C. Tenney: "Master the Master's life." (In fact, as I noted in the preface, the series of messages that gave rise to this book occurred one year into a sermon series on the Gospel of Mark.) Three things stand out about the life of Jesus:

1. The serenity of His life—He was busy without being in a hurry.
2. The secret of that serenity—He was constantly withdrawing from the crowd into the wilderness to hear the voice of His Father.
3. The cross—it was looming large as He resolutely set His face toward Jerusalem.

To be a disciple of Jesus Christ, therefore, means to follow Him in this threefold dimension: having serenity, being rooted in regular listening and setting our face toward the cross. Being cross-focused means many things, but Paul makes it clear that in our daily lives it involves self-sacrifice—developing a renewed mind that refuses to cling to what we have, does not grasp for what we don't have and will not exploit others but instead serves them (see Philippians 2:5-11). Oswald Chambers acknowledged the radical nature of this facet of discipleship when he said:

> There is an aspect of Jesus that chills the heart of a disciple to the core and makes the whole spiritual life gasp for breath. This strange Being with His face "set like a flint" and His striding determination, strikes terror into me. He is no longer Counselor and Comrade, He is taken up with a point of view I know nothing about, and I am amazed at Him.[5]

That's what it means to become a disciple.

Guinness also uses the word *apprenticeship*. Discipleship is a lifelong apprenticeship under Jesus Christ. How do we apprentice under Jesus? We do it first of all by exposing ourselves regularly to the Gospels (both in our own personal study and by sitting under good Bible preaching and teaching) so that the life and teachings of our Lord are reinforced in our lives. But I'm convinced that another critically important link is to apprentice under a mature follower of Jesus Christ.

Jesus was able to literally and directly apprentice His disciples in person, and He did it by spending time with them. He revealed Himself to them, He loved them, He gave them the word of God, He empowered them for ministry and He sent them out on their own mission. We can't literally and directly apprentice under Jesus, but we need other pilgrims who are walking on that path ahead of us and who will do for us what Jesus did for His disciples.

The input of a mentor is critical, as we can see from the example of Dwight D. Eisenhower. This great leader of the Allied invasion of Europe had a relatively undistinguished military career until he was placed under the command of General Fox Conner. Under Conner's guidance, Eisenhower's leadership and organizational skills began to bloom, until he grew into the great general, and later the great American president, whom we know of today. Eisenhower later wrote this eulogy to his mentor:

> Life with General Conner was a sort of graduate school in military affairs and the humanities, leavened by . . . a man who was experienced in his knowledge of men and their conduct. I can never adequately express my gratitude to this one gentleman. . . . But in a lifetime of association with great and good men, he is the one more or less invisible figure to whom I owe an incalculable debt.[6]

That's what mentoring does. On the other hand, what happens when we refuse to be mentored? In a somewhat humorous but equally powerful observation, Eugene Peterson tells how he once developed an interest in banjo playing. He picked up a banjo at a pawnshop, bought some instruction

books and learned a few tunes that he played with great glad-
ness. Over twenty years later, however, he wrote:

> Eventually I realized that if I was going to advance, I
> would have to get a teacher. It wasn't that I lacked
> knowledge—my stack of instruction books was now
> quite high. It wasn't that I lacked material—there were
> already far more songs in my books than I could ever
> learn well. But I didn't seem to be able to get the hang of
> it by just reading about them.
>
> I have not yet hired a teacher. It was never the right
> time. I procrastinated. I am still picking and singing the
> same songs I learned in the first few years. The crisp, glit-
> tering banjo sound that never failed to set feet tapping
> and laughter rippling now bores my wife and children to
> tears. I am not a little bored myself. I still intend to get a
> teacher.[7]

Eisenhower the leader, or Peterson the banjo player—it all
depends on our willingness to be apprenticed. We all fall into
one group or another—mentor or apprentice. To become like
Jesus in His serenity, in His ability to listen to the voice of God
and in His cross-focused servanthood, we need help. We can't
do it ourselves. The ruthless honesty that is needed to probe
our priority systems requires the help of a mentor. Look
around for someone you respect. And if you can't find someone, pray that God will bring him across your path. Sometimes
it can happen in a structured setting—within a small group, for
example. But it can happen in unstructured settings as well.

As we mature in the Christian life, we begin to mentor
even as we are being mentored. Look around for young men
and young women whom you can walk alongside; you have
walked longer on the pilgrim path, and you need to do for
them what Jesus did for His disciples. Spend time with them,
reveal yourself to them, love them, give them the Word of
God, empower them for ministry and then send them out to
do the work.

The third word I want to emphasize in Guinness' principle is *lifelong*. It is a lifelong apprenticeship under Jesus. We have to get rid of the retirement mentality when it comes to Christianity. If we're going to live integrated lives for Jesus Christ, we must acknowledge that there are no breaks in this process. We need breaks from our work, and even breaks from our closest relationships, to get our bearings. But to ask for a break from God and from learning to love God with all our hearts so that we can get our bearings in life is a contradiction in terms. Only a lifelong apprenticeship under Jesus will help us to become like Him and to act like He acts in all situations.

3. Calling

This kind of apprenticeship is hard work. What motivates us to persevere in the ruthless probing of our priorities, in choosing or being a mentor and in carrying on this process for a lifetime? That takes us to the third step: calling. *Calling is a compelling source of vision, discipline and accountability for every sphere of life.*

What is calling all about? Ravi Zacharias has said that no one really accomplishes anything significant for God until his heart is broken in some way. I know Ravi's heart was broken in India in the 1980s when he saw the plight of the pastors in Bombay and began to ask the question, *What am I going to leave behind?* World Vision started when Bob Pierce's heart was broken with the condition of abandoned children around the world. This issue of a broken heart is a thoroughly biblical concept. Listen to these Scriptures:

> Jeremiah 23:9: "Concerning the prophets: / My heart is broken within me . . . because of the LORD / and his holy words."

> Psalm 119:126, 136: "It is time for you to act, O LORD; / your law is being broken. . . . Streams of tears flow from my eyes, / for your law is not obeyed."

> Revelation 5:4: "I wept and wept because no one was found who was worthy to open the scroll or look inside."

> Nehemiah 1:4: "When I heard these things, I sat down and wept. For some days I mourned and fasted and prayed before the God of heaven."

You may say, "Of course we see brokenheartedness in such great spiritual giants as Jeremiah, David, John and Nehemiah. But does this principle apply to the average man or woman?" You'd better believe it. In Psalm 137—the original Babylonian blues of the Bible, by the way—we hear the brokenhearted cry of the exiles, ordinary people whose names we don't even know:

> By the rivers of Babylon we sat and wept
>   when we remembered Zion.
> There on the poplars
>   we hung our harps,
> for there our captors asked us for songs,
>   our tormentors demanded songs of joy;
>   they said, "Sing us one of the songs of Zion!"
> How can we sing the songs of the LORD
>   while in a foreign land?
> If I forget you, O Jerusalem,
>   may my right hand forget its skill.
> May my tongue cling to the roof of my mouth
>   if I do not remember you,
> if I do not consider Jerusalem
>   my highest joy.
>   (137:1-6)

The right hand was presumably the one used to play the harp, and the tongue, of course, was for singing. They were saying, "Let me lose my ability to sing and to play if I do not consider Jerusalem my highest joy."

Calling often comes out of a broken (or at least a strongly exercised) heart—a heart that God is beginning to squeeze a little so that we hurt with the things that "hurt" Him. Calling comes when our hearts are burdened with some need, and then we gradually become aware that we can meet that need. That's where our individual gifts, temperaments and passions begin to enter the picture.

What did Jesus say to Peter? "If you love me, feed my sheep" (see John 21:15-17)—exercise your gifts, do what I told you to do. Getting involved in the local church, understanding our gifts and learning where our passions lie—these are not optional if we want to live integrated lives, flowing out of hearts that love God.

This kind of calling becomes a source of vision, discipline and accountability. Vision certainly comes out of calling, and if my experience is any indication, God gradually develops that vision in our lives. It starts in skeletal form and then gets "fleshed out" over the years. Several examples come to mind.

A curriculum for spiritual training for leaders that I have been privileged to teach in so many parts of the world began in embryonic form in 1983 when a young man in our church came to the altar after I had finished the Sunday morning sermon and wanted his life to count for the kingdom. It turned into a call on me to mentor him. Out of that call came a vision for changed lives through one-on-one discipleship. The curriculum followed.

At about the same time, hundreds of miles away, a young engineer with a state utility company was challenged by a well-known Christian leader to devote his heart to studying and understanding his faith. That engineer responded to that call and started developing apologetics material in a format suitable for training others. It wasn't until eight years later, however, that God brought the two of us together to teach apologetics and spiritual disciplines as a team for several years.

Calling also becomes a source of discipline. The Apostle Paul declared, "Therefore I do not run like a man running aimlessly; I do not fight like a man beating the air." I have a goal. I have an aim. I have an enemy. "No, I beat my body and make it my slave so that after I have preached to others, I myself will not be disqualified for the prize" (1 Corinthians 9:26-27).

Much of our problem with the "disciplines," whether physical or spiritual, is that we try to accomplish them as ends in themselves, but they don't work that way. It is calling that becomes the source of discipline. I try to eat well, get enough sleep, get up early, exercise, study, read and think. Most of the time this discipline comes out of my sense of calling. Not as much as I would like it to, but a lot more than it used to and increasingly so.

Calling becomes a source of accountability as well. When we are willing to walk with somebody else and allow him to hold us accountable for this journey—that kind of courage can come only from a compelling sense of calling. Years ago, my wife and I spent several hours talking with a couple with whom we had just begun to share our spiritual journey. There was a reason that they were willing to be accountable, to spend so much time with us and to be vulnerable. I will never forget the husband's words spoken to me in the wee hours of the morning: "Sunder, I don't want to appear before God empty-handed on the day of judgment." That's the genesis of a compelling calling.

Calling and Secular Vocation

One problem that a layperson encounters when it comes to living out of a sense of calling is the apparent intrusion of one's secular vocation and other "daily grind" duties on one's time and energy. It seems so much easier for pastors to live an integrated life, because everything they do is in some way ostensibly "spiritual." Preaching, counseling, whatever—it's all ministry. But what if you're a teacher, a lawyer, a homemaker? How do you live an integrated life when so many hours of the week are taken up by work responsibilities? Does one have to quit one's secular job and go into so-called full-time ministry? Is that the only way one can live an integrated life?

Of course not. Jesus lived an integrated life as a carpenter for eighteen years. But we do need to think about our work in terms of this calling, which is our compelling source of vision, discipline and accountability; in terms of Christ invading and ordering and reordering our priorities; in terms of a lifetime apprenticeship under Jesus to become like Him. Eugene Peterson, in his book *Earth and Altar*, puts it this way:

> The test of our work is not the profit we gain from it or the status we receive from it but its effects in creation. Are persons impoverished? Is the land diminished? Is society defrauded? Is the world less or more because of my work? We have become so accustomed to evaluating work in terms of productivity that we have little sense of its meaning in terms of creativity. We have for so long asked the questions of efficiency and profit that it does not ever occur to us to ask the question of virtue. . . . God gives us work—not to further our ambition or to feather our nest but to deepen creation and sanctify society.[8]

And the key question he asks is "Is your work resulting in victims or celebrants?" Gordon MacDonald, in his book *Forging a Real-World Faith*, gives an example of how to get the right answer to that question.[9] The president of a company heard about a single mother who was struggling because her ex-husband wouldn't pay child support. So he found her a job in the telemarketing department, ensuring that she had flex-time hours so she could be with her children during most of their off-school hours. And MacDonald, as her pastor, watched her gain an increasing sense of confidence that she could meet her obligations and not have to go on welfare or make choices that might bring short-term relief but long-term disaster. That company president had turned a victim into a celebrant.

In a totally different context, I once read in *Leadership* magazine the words of a young writer in a publishing house, expressing his appreciation for his boss, senior editor Harold Myra. While editors he had previously worked for had written harsh, overly critical comments on his hard copy, Myra would write things like, "Try this," or "Perhaps you could add something to this," or "Maybe you'd like to rethink this paragraph." Myra's suggestions helped him improve his writing without making him feel belittled. His editorial comments produced a celebrant, not a victim.

I trust that I have given you a plumb line as to what an integrated life looks like. If we are loving God with all our hearts and our hearts are being increasingly united and undivided, then we can expect the kingdom of God—God's here-and-now rule—to order and reorder our lives' priorities and perspectives. We can expect that discipleship will become a lifetime apprenticeship under Jesus that teaches us to live as He would live if He were us. And we can expect our calling to be a compelling source of vision, discipline and accountability for every sphere and every stage of life. This is the integrated life.

Notes

1. Reginald Bibby, *Fragmented Gods: The Poverty and Potential of Religion in Canada* (Toronto: Irwin, 1987), passim.
2. Os Guinness and John Seel, eds., *No God But God: Breaking with the Idols of Our Age* (Chicago: Moody, 1992).
3. There are other metaphors for our relationship with Christ: Christ as our older brother, our high priest, etc. But He is Lord and Master, and that is the metaphor that is most relevant at this point.
4. John Greenleaf Whittier, "Dear Lord and Father of Mankind," *Hymns of the Christian Life* (Camp Hill, PA: Christian Publications, Inc., 1978), 154.
5. Oswald Chambers, *My Utmost for His Highest*, March 15.
6. Dwight D. Eisenhower, *At Ease: Stories I Tell to Friends* (Garden City, NY: Doubleday, 1967), p. 187.
7. Eugene Peterson, *Working the Angles: The Shape of Pastoral Integrity* (Grand Rapids, MI: Eerdmans, 1990), pp. 169-70.
8. Eugene Peterson, *Earth and Altar* (Downers Grove, IL: InterVarsity, 1985), p. 129.
9. Gordon MacDonald, *Forging a Real-World Faith* (Nashville: Thomas Nelson, 1989), p. 203.

5. A Theology of the Mind

Elton Trueblood, a wise and godly Christian leader of years gone by, said, "There are three areas that must be cultivated if any faith is to be a living faith: the inner life of devotion, the intellectual life of rational thought, and the outer life of human service."[1] Now, where he got that pithy summary from, I don't know. But it happens to correspond perfectly to the answer that the Lord Jesus Christ gave to the question "Of all the commandments, which is the most important?" (Mark 12:28), which was, "Love the Lord your God with all your heart and with all your soul and with all your mind and with all your strength . . . [and] love your neighbor as yourself" (12:30-31).

Loving God with all our hearts is the "inner life of devotion." Loving our neighbor as ourselves is the "outer life of service." And loving God with all our minds is the "intellectual life of rationality." So far we've explored the inner life of devotion—loving God with all our hearts. Now I would like to take a look at our intellectual lives. What does it mean to love God with all our minds?

The first reaction of some people to this dimension of our love for God is, "Well, if you're talking about studying and reading, I'm sorry, but that's not for me." To them, loving God with all one's mind is merely the hobbyhorse of a few people who are inclined in that direction; the rest of us can forget about it. It's a natural reaction but also dangerous and unwise. I am convinced that all of us need to develop our intellectual lives to the glory of God.

Let's take a look at the biblical basis for what I would like to call a "theology of the mind." The Bible has over 300 references to the mind and thinking, but they generally fall into several categories that, when taken together, provide us with a clear theology of the mind that can serve as a solid foundation for loving the Lord with all our minds. Let's begin by looking at what the Bible calls the natural mind and what happens to it at regeneration.

The Mind: Old and New

In Second Corinthians 4:4 we read, "The god of this age has blinded the minds of unbelievers, so that they cannot see the light of the gospel." And in Ephesians 4:17-18, Paul warns us to "no longer live as the Gentiles do, in the futility of their thinking . . . darkened in their understanding." The mind of every human being in his or her natural state is described as blind and his thinking as futile—achieving nothing significant from an eternal perspective. How did our minds get that way?

Romans 1:21 answers that question: "For although they knew God, they neither glorified him as God nor gave thanks to him, but their thinking became futile and their foolish hearts were darkened." Humans in their natural state refused to honor the God they knew, so their thinking became futile and their minds dark. Paul asserts that this results in an inevitable downward spiral into foolish idolatry: "They exchanged the truth of God for a lie, and worshiped and served created things rather than the Creator" (1:25).

But when the Holy Spirit of God grants us repentance, instills faith and regenerates us, look what happens to this natural mind. Jeremiah 31:33, which is repeated in Hebrews 10:16, says, "This is the covenant I will make with [them]. . . .

I will put my law in their minds and write it on their hearts."
And Ephesians 4:22-23 says, "You were taught, with regard
to your former way of life . . . to be made new in the attitude
of your minds." God has taken this darkened, futile and ignorant mind and, through His Holy Spirit, made it capable
of being renewed in knowledge, righteousness and holiness
as the law of God is progressively written on the mind.

In light of what He has done in the realm of our minds,
God gives us clear commands about our minds, such as "Set
your minds on things above, not on earthly things" (Colossians 3:2) and "Be transformed by the renewing of your
mind" (Romans 12:2). He has taken a darkened, futile and
ignorant mind and made it not new but capable of being renewed. That's our job—to take renewable minds and make
them progressively new.

The Battle for Our Minds

But this task is not easy, because we have an enemy scheming against us. Paul tells us, "Put on the full armor of God so
that you can take your stand against the devil's schemes"
(Ephesians 6:11). The word translated "schemes" in this verse
carries with it the idea of method or strategy. However, Paul
also writes, "For we are not unaware of his [Satan's] schemes"
(2 Corinthians 2:11). Here the word *schemes* comes from the
root word for "mind." Taken together, these two verses seem
to imply that Satan's fundamental strategy, his most insidious
move against us, is in the realm of our minds. Our minds are
the primary bull's-eye that the enemy is aiming for. Sometimes
he does this directly, often through individuals in his service.
At other times he does it through the surrounding culture,
whose collective mind-set Satan has shaped.

Examples of Satan's direct attacks on our minds are seen in
Paul's warnings against false teachers: "I am afraid that just as
Eve was deceived by the serpent's cunning, your minds may

somehow be led astray from your sincere and pure devotion to Christ" (2 Corinthians 11:3); "by smooth talk and flattery they deceive the minds of naive people" (Romans 16:18). Paul tells us that individuals, especially those holding credentialed and authorized positions as teachers, may be used by Satan to deceive the minds of even the most sincere and devoted believers, who are simply "naive"—not stupid, just not well taught in the ways of the Lord.

An example of Satan's use of the culture to get at our minds is evident in Peter's response when Jesus spoke to the disciples for the first time about the cross: " 'Never, Lord!' he said. 'This shall never happen to you!' " (Matthew 16:22). One likely factor governing Peter's response was the prevailing Jewish opinion about the nature of the Messiah. He was influenced by his culture. And who was the one ultimately behind this cultural influence? Look at Jesus' response: "Get behind me, Satan! You . . . do not have in mind the things of God, but the things of men" (16:23). Jesus declared that the culture that influenced Peter was in turn influenced by the father of lies.

Because of this opposition to the task of renewing our minds, God has called us to spiritual warfare and given us weapons with which to fight:

> The weapons we fight with are not the weapons of the world. On the contrary, they have divine power to demolish strongholds. We demolish arguments and every pretension that sets itself up against the knowledge of God, and we take captive every thought to make it obedient to Christ. (2 Corinthians 10:4-5)

To get a better handle on what Paul is saying here, we have to look at first-century warfare.

In those days, most cities were surrounded by massive walls. At strategic points along the perimeter of the walls, lofty towers were erected. Military strategists would retreat to these towers and from their vantage point be able to look around and direct the counterattack against the enemy forces. Conquering a city consisted of breeching the walls, taking the towers and capturing the military strategists. Once that was accomplished, taking the rest of the city captive was relatively easy.

Paul takes these familiar realities of literal war and applies them to spiritual warfare, but in reverse. Imagine the mind, in the natural, unregenerate state, as a city that the enemy has taken over, with walls and towers erected around that mind. At conversion, by the regenerative work of the Spirit, our minds have been made capable of being renewed by God, but at any given time, portions, even large portions, are still under enemy control. Our job is to use the weapons of our warfare to assault our minds and take them back for God.

What are the walls and towers around our minds? They are what Paul calls "arguments and pretensions"—habitual rationalizations by which we have excused our disobedience and maintained ungodly ways of thinking. They may be entrenched because of traumatic events in our pasts or by continual, deliberate acts of disobedience. All of these contribute to the building of walls that set themselves up against the knowledge of God. These are the "strongholds" we have to identify and tear down. If we do that, Paul says, our ordinary, daily thoughts (and the actions that flow out of them) will be relatively easy to take captive.

To encourage us in the battle, God has given us not only weapons but a promise. When Jesus walked the road to Emmaus with the two disciples, expounding to them all that concerned Him in the Scriptures, they later said, "Were not our hearts burning within us while he talked with us on the road and opened the Scriptures to us?" (Luke 24:32). But later on it says, "Then he opened their minds so they could understand the Scriptures" (24:45). The resurrected Lord Jesus Christ not only inflames our hearts but also instructs our minds with the Scriptures. Burning hearts and instructed minds are what God promises us if we will set our minds on things above, obey the commandments and enter into this warfare to repossess our minds, tearing down strongholds and taking every thought captive to make it obedient to Jesus Christ.

This is the skeleton of a biblical theology of the mind. To "flesh out," as it were, this skeleton, some questions need to be answered. What does this fight for our minds look like? What are some of the dimensions of this fight? As we answer these questions, we will enlarge our understanding of what it means to love God with all our minds.

Looking at the Christian Church today, it seems that Satan is winning this battle for our minds. Os Guinness and John Seel, in their book *No God But God*, make this stinging analysis of evangelicalism's poverty of mind:

> Contemporary evangelicals are no longer people of truth. Only rarely are they serious about theology. Both problems are a tragedy beyond belief. . . . Vaporized by critical theories, obscured by clouds of euphemism and jargon, outpaced by rumor and hype, overlooked for style and image, and eroded by advertising, truth in America is anything but marching on. . . .
>
> Worse still, the Protestant principle of *sola scriptura* [Scripture alone] is no longer operative in much of evangelicalism. Adherence to formal orthodoxy is still strong, but such modern sources of authority as politics, psychology, and management theory routinely eclipse biblical authority in practice. The combined effect is to render unthinkable the notion of an evangelical community that is defined by truth, united by truth and guided by truth.[2]

Guinness and Seel end this analysis by saying, "It is impossible to love God and not be a theologian."[3] Think about that statement. Is that true, or is it the wild exaggeration of someone who happens to like theology? Can we support from

Scripture that it is impossible to love God without being a theologian?

An Undivided Mind

To answer these questions, I want to begin with an observation from an earlier chapter. As we looked at loving God with all our hearts, we saw the need for an undivided heart, which naturally leads to an integrated life. The same is true when it comes to loving God with our minds. The Bible speaks often about the need to integrate our divided minds, using various images to reinforce the idea. For example, James refers to the one who doubts in prayer as "a double-minded man, unstable in all he does" (James 1:8).

The immediate context of this passage is asking God for wisdom. A double-minded man or woman, therefore, describes one who is not predisposed to confess that God alone is wise and who always has backup options in case he doesn't like what God tells him in answer to his prayers.

Later in his letter, James says, "Come near to God and he will come near to you. Wash your hands, you sinners, and purify your hearts, you double-minded" (4:8). There's the heart and the mind linked together again. And the call to purify ourselves from double-mindedness is in the context of quarreling and fighting with one another, which James 3:15 says is a mark of earthly, satanic wisdom.

How do we develop integrated, undivided minds? One clue is found in Psalm 119:113: "I hate double-minded men, / but I love your law." Part of loving God with all our hearts, you may remember, is learning to love the law of the Lord; a parallel process seems to be involved in seeking to love God with all our minds. It involves developing an understanding of the law of the Lord in such a way that our minds become more and more like the mind of Jesus Christ, influencing every aspect of our lives.

What a contrast to the way that so many of us live. Our understanding of the Bible is fragmentary. How many times have you heard a Christian say, "Doesn't it say somewhere in the Bible that . . ."? A little fragment here, a little piece there, and out of that patchwork we develop entire theologies by which we can determine the way we think and, hence, live. The psalmist, on the other hand, calls us to cure our double-mindedness by loving *all* of God's law, thereby developing the integrated mind of Christ.

Another Bible term for a divided mind is *corrupt*, as seen in the following passage:

> If anyone teaches false doctrines and does not agree to the sound instruction of our Lord Jesus Christ and to godly teaching, he is conceited and understands nothing. He has an unhealthy interest in controversies and quarrels . . . that result in envy, strife, malicious talk, evil suspicions and constant friction between men of *corrupt mind*, who have been robbed of the truth and who think that godliness is a means to financial gain. (1 Timothy 6:3-5)

Paul is warning Timothy that conceit, divisiveness and quarreling, as well as a materialistic approach to life, are directly related to unsound doctrine that robs us of the truth. What's the cure? Theology—the "sound instruction" of Christ that can take a corrupt mind and make it integrated again.

Paul also uses the word *unspiritual* to describe the divided mind of a heretic in Colossians 2:18-19: "Such a person goes into great detail about what he has seen, and his *unspiritual mind* puffs him up with idle notions. He has lost connection with the Head [Christ]."

It is interesting that nearly all of the heresies that the early Church encountered attacked the nature and person of the Lord Jesus Christ. They "lost connection with the Head" and began promoting such errors as gnosticism (which has been making a comeback in our day, under carefully disguised forms). At the cost of oversimplification for the avid student of historical theology, gnosticism taught that one needed to be initiated into an inner circle of those who had special insight into the nature and being of Jesus Christ (who, they said, was not God but a "demiurge," an intermediary in a series of emanations linking God and humans). This is one example of what Paul terms an unspiritual mind.

And so, whether it's double-mindedness, a corrupt mind or an unspiritual mind, the solution in every case seems to be the same: a love for the law of the Lord, for doctrine and for truth (especially concerning Jesus, the Living Word of God) that integrates that mind. These passages make this point negatively (i.e., don't have the divided mind of a doubter, a false teacher or a heretic). The point is also stated very positively, however, in several portions of Scripture where we are called to be sound, practical theologians.

In Isaiah, for example, there is a long section in chapters 44 through 46 that talks about the sovereignty of God over the nations of the world—particularly His ability to use the leaders of nations to accomplish deliverance and restoration for His people. The passage concludes with this statement: "Remember this, fix it in mind, / take it to heart, you rebels" (Isaiah 46:8). This verse specifically calls us to fix in our minds the doctrine of the sovereignty of God.

In Isaiah 26:3 we read these familiar words: "You will keep in perfect peace / him whose mind is steadfast, / because he trusts in you." It is a verse that is often quoted and sung. What is amazing, however, is the context of that statement. Later on in the chapter we read, "We were with child, we writhed in pain, / but we gave birth to wind. / We have not brought salvation to the earth; / we have not given birth to people of the world. / But your dead will live; / their bodies will rise" (26:18-19). This steadfastness of mind comes in the midst of a national defeat! Israel has failed to be a channel of God's glory to the nations, and yet, somehow, Isaiah is exhorting God's people to steadfastness in the midst of that failure. Such steadfastness can come only from an unshakable conviction about the sovereignty of God and His power—which together assure us that He will accomplish His purposes even in the midst of national failure.

I don't know how one can get that kind of conviction without a saturation of the mind and the heart with the Word of God and the work of God in the world that repeatedly evidences the truth of Isaiah 46 and 26.

But perhaps the bluntest statement of this truth was penned by Paul to the Corinthians. The church in that city thought that, when it came to spirituality, they had arrived. They took pride in their unbridled "freedom" as "super-wise" Christians and were second to none in the multiplicity and richness of spiritual gifts.

But they were lousy practitioners of the Christian life. Look at the many problems that characterized the Corinthian church: quarreling and divisions; hero worship (preferring one Christian leader over another); lack of church discipline (tolerating gross sins like incest); lawsuits between Christians; the exercise of liberty in gray areas even when it endangered the spiritual growth of immature believers; problems relating to divorce, remarriage and desertion; impropriety and outright lack of love for the poor among them when it came to their "love feasts," linked to the celebration of the Lord's Supper; doctrinal confusion (especially about the Resurrection); and disagreements about spiritual gifts and how to apply them. They were incredibly rich, incredibly free, but they didn't know how to translate that into a life marked by love and purity.

So Paul says to them, "Brothers, stop thinking like children. In regard to evil be infants, but in your thinking be adults" (1 Corinthians 14:20). This is a clarion call to become sound, practical theologians by cultivating a disciplined mind. Christians—

all of us, not just a few leaders—should be able to take doctrines such as the sovereignty of God and the Resurrection, for
example, and apply them to nitty-gritty, everyday situations of
life.

It would seem to me, therefore, that Guinness is right—it
is not possible to love God without becoming, in some form
or another, a theologian. We should be systematically training our minds to be integrated by all of the law of the Lord.

Not Cut Out for This?

At this point, you may be saying, "OK, maybe theology is
for all of us, but I don't have what it takes. I don't have the
gifts, the intellectual capacity, the opportunity to study."
Paul anticipated this, so he gave the Corinthians this word of
encouragement (probably to prepare them for his stinging rebuke later in the letter):

> We have not received the spirit of the world but the Spirit
> who is from God, that we may understand what God has
> freely given us. This is what we speak, not in words taught
> us by human wisdom but in words taught by the Spirit,
> expressing spiritual truths in spiritual words. . . . But we
> have the mind of Christ. (1 Corinthians 2:12-13, 16)

In other words, Paul is saying, "I have the Holy Spirit of
God. I am speaking inspired truths to you—the truths of the
Bible. And you are spiritual men and women who have the
mind of Christ; therefore, you can understand the truth of
the Spirit taught in the words of the Spirit by teachers of the
Spirit."

The amazing thing is that Paul penned these words to a
messy, problem-riddled church made up of former male prosti-
tutes, swindlers, gamblers, drunkards. Paul reminds them,
"And that is what some of you were. But you were washed, you
were sanctified, you were justified" (6:11). There isn't a single
Christian who cannot become a theologian and learn to love

God with his or her mind, because Christians have the mind of Christ. You may not become a teacher or a preacher. You may never write texts on systematic theology. But you can learn to love God with your mind and integrate it systematically.

Last Days Urgency

Finally, Scripture makes it clear that this whole business of having an integrated mind cannot be approached casually. There is an inescapable note of urgency in the Bible when it speaks about this particular topic, all related to Christ's return. Many verses that call us to a renewed mind and right thinking are linked to the Second Coming.

For example, Revelation 17 speaks of imminent judgment upon Babylon, a city that throughout Scripture is a symbol of secular culture, anti-Christian government and pagan religion. How does this description of impending judgment conclude? "This calls for a mind with wisdom" (17:9).

Peter also sounds a similar theme, calling us to right thinking as we await Christ's return: "Therefore, prepare your minds for action . . . set your hope fully on the grace to be given you when Jesus Christ is revealed" (1 Peter 1:13); "the end of all things is near. Therefore be clear minded and self-controlled so that you can pray" (4:7). Of course, a major theme of both his letters is the second coming of Jesus Christ. In Peter's second letter, he tells us his purpose for writing: "Dear friends, this is now my second letter to you. I have written both of them as reminders to stimulate you to wholesome thinking" (2 Peter 3:1). What does he mean by "wholesome thinking"? Later in the letter we find out as he warns us not to give in to the discouragement and skepticism of scoffers who deny that Christ is coming again—in a specific instance of the influence of the cultural mind-set that wars against an integrated mind.

The writer of Hebrews, after listing numerous heroes of faith, subscribes to the same kind of thinking:

> All these people were still living by faith when they died.
> . . . And they admitted that they were aliens and strang-
> ers on earth. People who say such things show that they
> are looking for a country of their own. *If they had been
> thinking* of the country they had left, they would have
> had opportunity to return. Instead, they were longing for
> a better country—a heavenly one. (11:13-16)

There is a similar focus in Paul's well-known words:

> But one thing I do: Forgetting what is behind and strain-
> ing toward what is ahead, I press on toward the goal to
> win the prize for which God has called me heavenward in
> Christ Jesus.
> All of us who are mature should take such a view of
> things. And *if on some point you think differently*, that too
> God will make clear to you. (Philippians 3:13-15)

What are all these verses saying? They demonstrate a certain mind-set, a certain way of thinking. And they exhort us all
to think that way in the light of the coming of Jesus Christ, described as a present urgency. If the time was short 2,000 years
ago, it is even shorter today. What is that mind-set? Simply this:
In light of the certainty of Christ's coming, and the uncertainty
of the time of His coming, we need to be clear-minded people
who think straight. Why? So we can pray with wisdom, so we
can bear up under the increasing persecution and mental seduc-
tion of the culture, so we can be loosely attached to the things of
this world like the people in Hebrews who looked for, thought
about and hence longed for a different country and so we can,
like Paul, press on toward the heavenly prize that awaits us.

By the way, this also underlines a seldom emphasized truth—
that the fundamental purpose of prophecy is not to stimulate
all kinds of speculative thinking about the future but to light a
fire under lazy, undisciplined and divided minds so that we
can think clearly and act properly when the prophesied last
days suddenly come upon us.

So, where do we go from here? I haven't given any practical suggestions in this chapter, but that was deliberate. If I had given you a list of what to study and what to read, you might have worked on it for a week or two and then given up. To have a lifelong motivation to love God with all our minds as well as our hearts requires nothing less than an unshakable conviction from the Word of God about what our minds are intended to be. That is why I've taken all these biblical passages on the mind and set them before you.

And just in case you've lost the big picture in the midst of all these verses, let me quickly summarize my version of a theology of the mind: The natural mind is darkened, futile and ignorant. God has regenerated that mind to make it capable of being progressively renewed in knowledge, righteousness and holiness by the law of God. He has therefore commanded us to set our hearts on things that are above. But we have an opponent—Satan—whose strategies are mind-oriented and who works through individuals and culture. We have weapons by which we are called to tear down speculations, overturn strongholds and captivate thoughts. God has promised that as we do that, He will open our minds and give us burning hearts.

We learned that the cure for a double mind, a corrupt mind and an unspiritual mind is theology. Bad theology always results in an unintegrated mind. We are called instead to become sound, practical theologians, to stop thinking like children and to think like adults. And the urgency behind all this is Christ's certain return. Clear and wholesome thinking is needed so that we can pray, live holy lives and bear up under persecution.

There is only one practical response to this truth, and that is to make the critical decision that Daniel made, as acknowledged by an angelic visitor: "Do not be afraid, Daniel. Since the first day that you set your mind to gain understanding and to humble yourself before your God, your words were heard, and I have come in response to them" (Daniel 10:12). This is the challenge before you. Will you "set your mind to gain understanding and to humble yourself before God"? Will you become a theologian? Will you love God with all your mind?

Notes

1. Elton Trueblood, *Christianity Today*, February 14, 1969, p. 3.
2. Os Guinness and John Seel, eds., *No God But God: Breaking with the Idols of Our Age* (Chicago: Moody, 1992), pp. 18-9.
3. Ibid., p. 19.

6.
Confronting
Modernity

Two of the most prestigious magazines for preachers, *Preaching* and *Pulpit Digest*, did a very interesting analysis of 200 sermons preached in evangelical pulpits from the years 1985 through 1989.[1] They grouped these sermons into four broad categories. The first included sermons in which both the content and the organization came from the Bible; the second, in which the content came from the Bible but the organization was determined by the preacher's own preferences; the third, in which neither the content nor the organization came from the Scriptures but could be identifiably recognized as having to do with Christian matters; and the fourth, in which there was nothing explicitly recognizable as Christian (i.e., sermons that could have been preached at a Rotary Club luncheon by a secular professional).

Here's the statistical breakdown: Barely a quarter of the sermons had both the content and the organization determined by the Scriptures; twenty-two percent had the content determined by Scripture but with a free organization; and well over half of the sermons had neither the content nor the organization determined by the Scriptures!

Then they looked at these same sermons from another perspective: major orientation. How many of these sermons were not simply talks about God but were grounded explicitly in the character, nature and will of God? Barely twenty percent of the sermons met that criteria. What is the implication of findings like this?

David Wells, a professor of historical and systematic theology at Gordon Seminary, made this observation:

> The findings were, then, an attempt to measure the prevailing spirit of the age in today's pulpit. Is it anthropocentric, centered on human beings, or theocentric, centered on God? The overwhelming proportion of sermons—more than 80 percent—were anthropocentric. It seems that God has become a rather awkward appendage to the practice of evangelical faith. . . . He appears not to be at its center. The center, in fact, is typically the self. God . . . increasingly is understood within a therapeutic model of reality.
>
> If, in fact, these statistics bear any significant relation to what those in the pews are thinking, then we have the makings of a kind of faith . . . that is not much anchored in the character and greatness of God, and that is almost completely unaware of the culture in which it must live—for in virtually none of the sermons analyzed was any attempt made to take account of the modern situation.[2]

I would like to address his last point: that "virtually none" of the sermons—out of 200 preached in 4 years in evangelical pulpits—analyzed the modern mind-set.

The Spirit of Modernity

What is this thing called modernity?[3] How does it affect us, and why is it that so many evangelical pulpits have been taken over by the modern mind-set? If you find that this discussion stretches your mind a little more than you may be used to, it's quite appropriate, because we are learning to love God with our minds.

If I use more than my normal share of quotations, that too is appropriate, for if we're going to love God with our minds, we need to engage with the material that thought-provoking Christians are reading and writing, particularly to cure our cultural blindness. Of course, I'm hoping your interest will be piqued enough by these quotations to make you want to read the books from which this material is taken. That too is part of learning to love God with all our minds.

In the last chapter we learned that if we want to love God with all our minds, we have to become theologians. Now I hope to show you that we have to become sociologists and philosophers as well. There is no branch of study that is exempt or taboo for the Christian. The so-called cultural mandate in Genesis 1 (to rule and to subdue) makes that clear.

I would like to begin by asking a question: Why is it that so much of evangelical morality, and even so many of our political initiatives ("moral majority" campaigns, etc.), have so little effect upon culture? John Seel has this incisive, but troubling, observation:

> Evangelicals are slowly learning that cultural change is brought about by cultural gatekeepers—those people who have access to and control of the reality defining institution of America. Cultural gatekeepers give shape to what we take for granted about our worlds.[4]

The average person on the street doesn't get his philosophy from academic courses. It is molded at an unconscious level through media—TV, movies, the arts, theater, books. Those are the "cultural gatekeepers" of our society to whom Seel refers. He continues:

> Yet few evangelicals hold these positions of influence and few evangelical ministries seek to reach these people. Moreover few evangelicals have the cultural capital needed to address these gatekeepers. We are seriously disadvantaged by a crippling anti-intellectualism. Many evangelicals just do not think. For the first time in American history, the more one is educated the less likely it is that he or she will take

faith seriously. We seem to be gatekeeper proof. Evangelicals cannot count on their size alone. Numbers may win
elections, but minds win cultures.[5]

If we want to change the culture in which we live, the first
thing we need to do is to understand the culture and stop it
from influencing us. Until that happens we'll never influence
the prevailing culture for the kingdom of God. What is the
modern mind-set? How has it become so prevalent? How
does it encroach into the Christian life? And who are the carriers of modernity?

Modernity does not mean simply keeping up-to-date, like
when we say, "Modern science does not believe that the world
is flat" or "Many hospitals in Africa lack modern equipment."
I'm talking about the spirit of modernity. One definition I find
helpful is this: Modernity is the premise that the top-down
causation of God and the supernatural has been decisively re-
placed by the bottom-up causation of human designs and
products. In other words, it is the belief that God no longer ini-
tiates and controls the universe, but human beings do.

That is the essence of the modern mind-set. How has it become so prevalent? We need to consider that from two directions: the contribution of philosophy, the history of ideas;
and the contribution of sociology, the history of behavior.

Let's begin by looking at the contribution of philosophy. C.S.
Lewis refers to the French Revolution of the eighteenth century
as the "great divide" in Western civilization—the time before
which people thought Christianly and after which they started
thinking differently. Before then, the dominant worldview—in
the West, at least—was Christian. People thought in Christian
terms and categories. Even non-Christian writers, in order to
be understood, had to appear as Christians. Thomas Hobbes
wrote a book on political theory called *Leviathan*. Though he
was an atheist, the book was full of quotations from the Bible—
it was even written in King James English—because the public
wouldn't have understood it otherwise.

The eighteenth century ushered in the philosophy of deism, which contended that God made us but has revealed enough in nature for us to know what is good and right and necessary for a healthy, proper life; no further information (via revelation) is needed. Specifically, we do not need the God of the Bible.

Then came the nineteenth century, and with it the realization that nature has few models of what is "good" and "right." Instead they saw nature "red in tooth and claw," with survival of the fittest apparently being the order of the day. It was the century in which Charles Darwin wrote *Origin of the Species* and Friedrich Nietzsche triumphantly (if inaccurately) proclaimed, "God is dead." From now on, he said, men and women will be supermen and superwomen, human beings who define their own morality. No one will be able to tell another human being what is right and what is wrong.

And that's exactly what happened in the twentieth century—human beings defined their own morality. Might became right. Hitler read both Nietzsche and Darwin; they were major influences in his life—with colossally tragic consequences.

In summary, here's the history of ideas: Before the eighteenth century, God was alive and involved in human affairs; in the eighteenth century, the Bible was killed and a clear picture of God discarded; in the nineteenth century, God Himself was killed; and in the twentieth century, more humans have been killed by other humans than in all previous recorded history. This is the philosophical impetus behind modernity.

Secularization, Pluralization, Privatization

What about the sociological impetus? As we turn from the history of ideas to the history of human behavior, what do we see? In a series of taped lectures given over two decades ago, Os Guinness summed it up in three words: *secularization, pluralization* and *privatization*.

In those tapes, he defined *secularization* as the process by which religious ideas, institutions and interpretations have increasingly lost their social significance. The word *secular* comes from a Latin root that refers to church-owned land that was taken back by the state. That concept eventually came to refer to anything that was taken from the domain of religion into the domain of the state, including institutions, ideas and interpretations. This process has been going on for centuries so that today, in the Western world at least, we have a situation in which the natural world, not the supernatural, is accepted as the only "official" reality.

One of the contributors to or accelerators of this process of secularization is the development of science. As scientific knowledge increases, many things that were considered supernatural, mysterious or unexplainable now have natural explanations. From the movements of heavenly bodies to disease in human bodies, the supernatural seems less and less necessary as science continues to give natural explanations for various phenomena.

Another accelerator of secularization is officialdom—the opinion-molding institutions of society, including government, media and schools—to which most people have maximum exposure. Because officialdom pleads for ordinary reality as the only reality, it becomes an avenue for communicating that principle. And so through this process, successive layers of society have been removed from religious influences.

Guinness labeled the next sociological phenomenon as *pluralization*—the process by which several competing worldviews are made available to members within society and no one worldview is predominant. An accelerator of this is technology. Marshall McLuhan coined the term *global village* to describe how the world is "shrinking." Technology has made it possible for us to traverse the globe in very short periods of time so that many major North American cities have a diversity of cultures. And more North Americans are traveling to other cultures. Most of us regularly encounter people who live differently, think differently and act differently. Even if we never travel, we can turn on the TV and see a Buddhist temple in Thailand, an animistic celebration somewhere in Africa, an ancient Indian ritual in the Amazon jungle or Hindus worshiping in India.

Technology has done one more thing: It has concentrated in cities. The city is the place to go; that's where the action is. And over the last few decades we've seen a huge migration into the cities, which further multiplies our exposure to cultural options. And when faced with such a multiplicity of options, we begin to ask, "Just a minute; how do I know I'm right? How can I possibly claim that my current worldview is the only correct worldview? What if their view of looking at God is not the same as mine? What if they are right? What if their view of not believing in God at all is right? What if I believe these things only because my parents have taught me all of these things?" Pluralization begins to undercut the things we have believed, resulting in relativism, uncertainty, subjectivism and anxiety.

Guinness' third word that will help us understand the sociological impact of modernity is *privatization*—the process of separating the public and the private spheres of life. The same technology that has driven secularization and pluralization has also resulted in huge, impersonal organizations, large businesses and monstrous computers, making the public world into an anxious place. I'm just a number in a computer; I'm only a cog in the machine; I can't influence a huge corporation; my bosses are only concerned about the bottom line.

This makes the private sphere of my life increasingly important. Wait till I get back to my house, get out of my uniform and into my jeans—then you'll see what I'm *really* like. The private arena is where bureaucracy cannot touch me. But one of the consequences of this cleavage between public and private life is that religion has been consigned to the private sphere. Watch whatever you want on TV, believe what-

ever you want, do whatever you want on Sunday; but
*please—don't talk about it in the boardroom, the staff room, the uni-
versity lecture hall!* Don't bring it up at work; don't discuss it at
a sporting event. That's rude, that's insensitive, that's the
public arena; just keep it private.

Philosophical refinements progressively killed the Bible,
then God, then humans. Add to that this relentless march of
secularization, pluralization and privatization, and it's easy
to see how modernity, characterized by a "bottom-up" causation of human designs and human products, has completely eliminated the "top-down" causation of the supernatural God. And in the midst of such a culture, we are called
to live as disciples of Christ.

Christians have been asked for 2,000 years to live in tension—to be in the world but not of the world. Tragically, we
have attempted to resolve this tension by going to one of two
extremes. The first extreme is *isolation*. We are not *of* the
world; in fact, we are so far away from it that we are not *in*
it—we cannot influence it. The other danger is *compromise*.
We are very much *in* the world, but we are so much *of* the
world that we have no message to give it. The danger of past
centuries, even of past decades, was largely at the isolation
end of the spectrum. But without question, the major danger
nowadays is compromise—unthinkingly capitulating to the
spirit of modernity.

The Process of Compromise

How does the spirit of modernity infiltrate Christians?
What are the dynamics of compromise? I'm indebted again
to Os Guinness for his very helpful analysis of this problem.

He identifies four components to this infiltration—assumption, abandonment, adaptation and assimilation.[6]

The first step is assumption—some aspect of modern life or
thought is entertained as significant or superior to what I al-

ready know and therefore assumed to be true. The second step is abandonment—something traditional, of course, has to be discarded, i.e., everything that does not fit in with my new assumption. (By discarding what we already know, we are not simply changing tactics; we are rejecting truth.) In the third step, adaptation, whatever remains of traditional belief is adapted to fit into the new assumptions. The result is assimilation—the gospel has been assimilated to fit the shape of culture.

Let me illustrate this four-step process of compromise in two areas of current debate. One won't hit too close to home to "traditional" evangelicals, so I can probably discuss it without causing much discomfort. The other may be more irritating. But my goal here is not to debate or take a stand on either of these issues; I simply want to illustrate the process of compromise.

The first issue is homosexuality.

Assumption: I look around and see people who are ordinary human beings, though different from me. I understand that some of their sexual preferences may well be traceable to things that happened to them in their past. They certainly can't be blamed for that. And if the recent rumblings of some researchers eventually prove to be true, maybe there's a genetic basis[7] as well that further absolves them of responsibility. If all that is true, I certainly don't want to appear unenlightened and dull in front of all my peers. So it seems like a fairly good assumption to make that monogamous homosexuality may be quite all right.

Abandonment: If I'm a Christian, something traditional has to go. Everything in the Bible that explicitly condemns homosexuality as sinful has somehow got to be eliminated. So I will simply disregard those verses.

Adaptation: Other verses I may adapt, because abandonment is a pretty hard step, and if I can adapt without abandoning, so much the better. So I will say that God's judgment on Sodom and Gomorrah in Genesis 19 wasn't really because of their homosexuality but their lack of hospitality.

And when Paul says, "Men also abandoned natural relations with women and were inflamed with lust for one another" (Romans 1:27), I can assert that all he is condemning is *promiscuous* homosexuality; he doesn't say anything about *monogamous* homosexuality at all.

Assimilation: Finally, I end up with an assimilated gospel—homosexual ministers and homosexual churches, *all considered to be consistent with the historic gospel.* Assumption, abandonment, adaptation and assimilation—that's how they work together to subvert the claims of the gospel.

Now that particular issue is one on which many evangelicals have largely resented the pressure to compromise. One that hits a lot closer is the so-called gender bias of Scripture. How might the "4A" process identified by Guinness work in that area?

Assumption: We look around and say, "There's no difference between men and women except for the obvious biological ones. Both are made in the image of God and there ought to be absolutely no basis for differentiation in roles, functions, ministries, etc." It seems like a self-evident truth; therefore, we assume it.

Abandonment: We have to do some abandoning, maybe. (*Remember, I'm focusing on the process, not the specifics of the issue.*) What do I do with those sections from Paul's writings that seem to talk about gender differences that go beyond external, biological factors? Some people have chosen to abandon them by redefining Paul as a "rabbi." In other words, when Paul writes, "There is neither . . . male nor female" (Galatians 3:28), he is an inspired author of Scripture. But when he asks wives to submit to husbands or forbids women to teach men, then Paul is just a rabbi, simply reflecting the rabbinical teachings of his day, which often marginalized women. So we can ignore whole chunks of Pauline Scripture just by saying, "Paul was just a rabbi." That's abandonment.

Adaptation: How would adaptation look when applied to this subject? We simply redefine a lot of words. We redefine *headship* to mean "source," *obedience* to mean "listening," *submission* to mean _____ (I haven't heard of any new definitions yet). Thus the adaptation continues.

Assimilation: Finally, we have an assimilated gospel. One form of assimilation on this subject was driven home to me awhile ago when I was speaking at Camp of the Woods in Lake Speculator, New York. I had preached a series of messages on the foundations of Christian living. After the message on marriage from Ephesians 5, one young lady said to me, "Thank you so much for not avoiding that passage. I've grown weary of listening to preachers totally bypass what Ephesians 5 has to say whenever they talk about marriage." Avoiding passages of Scripture that might be "offensive" to some is an assimilated gospel.

Am I saying that the Church need not look at women's issues very seriously? No. Am I denying the injustices of the past or suggesting that there have not been distortions of biblical passages on this issue? Of course not. I'm merely illustrating the way in which the "4A" process can work to infiltrate the gospel. The point I want to emphasize is that we should not tackle controversial issues by the process of assumption, abandonment, adaptation and assimilation. We should do it instead by facing the reality of the biblical data as well as the reality of human life—and, through humility, prayer, integrity, forgiveness and risk-taking, live out the tension of being *in* but not *of* the world. Let us beware! If in the cause of "right" we adopt a wrong process ("4A" is one of many), without knowing it we have been molded by the mind-set of modernity.

Like a Disease

Let's take a step back and summarize what we have learned so far. An analogy to disease may be helpful. If we want to prevent malaria, for example, we need to understand what malaria is. We did this by defining modernity. Then of course we need to understand the conditions under which malaria spreads: swamps, stagnant water, etc. Those are equivalent to the philosophical and sociological processes that molded modernity. Then we need to understand what happens when the malaria germ gets into our bodies. That's the dynamics of compromise.

But no study of malaria is complete without studying mosquitoes, the carriers of malaria. And there are "mosquitoes" of modernity as well—six categories of people. And just as not all mosquitoes carry malaria, not all people who fall under these categories are carriers of modernity. This is a distinction that we need to keep in mind.

Guinness and Seel, in their book *No God But God*, identify these six carriers of modernity.[8] First of all, there are the *pundits*, the experts for whom everything can be known; their goal is information. Then come the *engineers*, for whom everything can be designed; their goal is production. Then there are the *marketers*, for whom everything can be positioned and sold; their goal is consumer satisfaction. Next we have the *consultants*, for whom everything can be organized; their goal is management. Close on their heels we find the *therapists*, for whom everything can be treated; their goal is healing. And finally, there are the *impresarios*, for whom everything can be conveyed through images (no matter reality); their goal is public relations. These are the six "mosquitoes" of modernity about whom we have to be careful.

As I noted above, not every person in these categories carries the disease. I was trained as an engineer and worked at Atomic Energy of Canada for eleven years, but I sure hope I am not a "modernity mosquito." But if anybody carries modernity's infection, it's likely to come from one of these sources.

For example, an illustration of the pundit combined with the impresario is the ubiquitous TV talk show host or hostess. Once her makeup artists primp her up perfectly, there is no subject that she can't pronounce on—and with believable authority. She has an opinion on everything. As noted in one essay from *No God But God*, "Informed opinion in America has become the replay of yesterday's talk show."[9]

How about the marketer? How has marketing affected Christianity? These are actual quotations taken from Christian books on church growth:

> The Church is a business. . . . Marketing is essential for a business to operate successfully. . . . The Bible is one of the world's great marketing texts. . . . The Bible does not warn against the evils of marketing. . . . So it behooves us not to spend time bickering about techniques and processes. . . . Think of your church not as a religious meeting place, but as a service agency—an entity that exists to satisfy people's needs.[10]

And then this one, probably the most blatant:

> It is critical . . . that we keep in mind a fundamental principle of Christian communication: the audience, not the message, is sovereign.[11]

That's the extent to which marketing has brought modernity into the Church. For an illustration of the consultant or therapist, I want to cite some statistics noted by David Wells, who looked at a key journal addressed to Christian leaders. He analyzed articles appearing in that journal over a nine-year period; this is what he found:

> A survey of all the essays from 1980 to 1988 in this journal shows that less than 1 percent made any obvious attempt to root the answers in anything biblical or doctrinal—despite the fact that many of the problems . . . are addressed directly in Scripture. Instead, the answers were taken heavily from the insights of the managerial and therapeutic revolutions. . . . The two cultural characters that capture what is most important in modernity are the psychologist and the manager [two of the "mosquitoes" listed earlier]. These characters now define what the professionalized pastor is becoming: in the pul-

pit, a psychologist whose business is to spread warm feelings; in the study, a CEO whose business is to have a
successful year in terms of numbers.[12]

Behind all of this is our archenemy, Satan, subversively
shaping large segments of the culture around us and, as we
learned in the preceding chapter, attempting to shape our
mind-sets. Loving God with all our minds involves winning
the battle for our minds, not only by becoming theologians
(as we learned in the preceding chapter) but by gaining a
good grasp of the sociological and philosophical dynamics
shaping our surrounding culture. Then we can do a much
more thorough job of pulling down the strongholds and taking every thought captive to make it obedient to Jesus Christ
(2 Corinthians 10:4-5). The next time you are bitten by a
mosquito, let it remind you of something far more deadly
that is all around us—modernity.

Notes

1. David Wells, in Os Guinness and John Seel, eds., *No God But God: Breaking with the Idols of Our Age* (Chicago: Moody, 1992), pp. 184-5.
2. Ibid., p. 185.
3. I know that we are now well into a postmodern society and so discussing modern-ism may seem anachronistic at this time. But keep in mind that (a) the research being cited was conducted before postmodernism became a buzzword; (b) postmodernism, in its popular, "street-level" form, is arguably a version of mod-ernism; (c) many people, even those just out of university, still show every sign of being infected by modernism; and (d) the purpose of this message is to illustrate one dimension of what it means to think fiercely as Christians, and modernism will serve just as well as postmodernism for that.
4. John Seel (headmaster, The Cambridge School of Dallas), *The Evangelical Melt-down: Modernity and the Hysteresis Habitus*, doctoral dissertation, University of Maryland, 1992.
5. Ibid.
6. Guinness, *No God But God*, pp. 166-7.
7. Nine years after this sermon was preached, a "gay" gene has yet to be isolated.
8. Guinness, *No God But God*, pp. 171-2.
9. Ibid., p. 172.
10. Ibid., p. 167.
11. Ibid., pp. 167-8.
12. David Wells, in Guinness, *No God But God*, p. 181.

7.

Remembering the Past

In the film *Dances with Wolves*, Kevin Costner plays a Civil War hero who is sent to command an outpost on the Western frontier. He makes friends with a nearby group of Sioux Indians, whom he finds to be far more attractive than many of the white people he knows. Charles Colson has a penetrating analysis of this film in his book *The Body*, in which he points out that the Sioux are consistently portrayed as "noble and humane," while all the white men (except Costner, of course) are "drunken, insane, perverted, or vicious."

The historical fact that the Sioux were among the most violent of all the native North American tribes is blatantly ignored in the film, and while no one can deny that many white people abused the Indians, the one-sided portrayal in the film sends a clear message, Colson says, that "in both nuanced allusions as well as out-and-out caricature, the noble savage's enemy is Judeo-Christian civilization."[1]

Welcome, brothers and sisters, to an academic philosophy known as deconstructionism. What is it? Colson defines it as a wholesale rejection of objective truth, which means that all interpretations of history, law and politics are to be considered biased. As such, there is no such thing as "historical fact," since every event or written report of that event is just another person's opinion or interpretation. Deconstructionists believe, Colson says, that "past events or writings have no intrinsic meaning. . . . So we freely revise the past to conform to current politically correct values.[2]

This is another illustration of how a philosophy hammered out in the hallowed halls of academia finds its way almost unconsciously into the fabric of our being through movies, the arts, etc. The subtler the art form, the more subversive, and hence the more thorough the deconstruction.

But why this attempt to debunk history? Because academia, Hollywood and other cultural gatekeepers of our society know very well that history is the greatest antidote to the disease of modernity. The sad part, though, is how successful the deconstructionists have been in infiltrating evangelical society. Consider this excerpt from a letter written by a graduate of an evangelical seminary, writing about his school:

> [My professors considered writers] such as Aquinas, Augustine, Calvin, and Luther to be interesting, but not as important as modern theologians. In fact, it appears that contemporary evangelicals are "embarrassed" at the notion of espousing and teaching classical theology. One . . . professor told me that men such as Aquinas and Calvin were great for their day, but their writings are no longer that substantial. The overall feeling . . . is that students need to spend more time in modern theology. This is a tragic shift that seems to be taking place throughout the evangelical community. Over and over again, I've encountered evangelicals who are so enamored by the "newness" of modern theological ideas that they abandon the real giants whose writings have stood for centuries.[3]

If we are going to love God with all our minds, not only do we need to develop an understanding of the disease of modernity, but we also need to develop a love for its greatest antidote—history. Os Guinness, in his book *No God But God*, says it persuasively:

> The possibility of a vital thrust forward depends on a vital thrust back. Evangelicals are, in part, children of moder-

nity. But if we are not to be made spiritual orphans of modernity, we must nourish faith and deepen gratitude
through appreciation of the great centuries of vital orthodoxy and "what has been believed always by all Christians
everywhere." If we are not to be victims of fashionable-
ness, superficiality and hysteria, we need the antidote of a
collective memory.[4]

Guinness notes further what "remembering the past" can
give us: identity, faith, wisdom, renewal and dynamism. While
he did not elaborate on each of these, let me "rush in where angels fear to tread" and take a closer look at each.

Identity

If there is one thing that Church history has taught me, it is
the truth of Jesus' words: "I will build my church, and the gates
of Hades will not overcome it" (Matthew 16:18). The Church
has proven indestructible for 2,000 years. One of the first
things I did when I came on staff at Rexdale Alliance Church in
October 1980 was to take a seminary course in historical theology. I will never cease to be grateful for what I learned in
those four months. I was introduced to the writings of the early
Church fathers and how they hammered out the various
creeds that many Christians so often repeat almost mechani-
cally. They wrote them to prevent the encroachment of hereti-
cal doctrines that questioned, for example, the humanity of
the Lord Jesus Christ while overemphasizing His deity, or vice
versa.

I was especially thrilled when we studied Athanasius,
known for his grand declaration, *Athanasius Contra Mundum*—
"Athanasius against the whole world"—because he said that
Jesus Christ is both God and man. I marveled at the grace of
God in the life of Augustine, who memorably described himself in his pre-conversion state as a man who scratched the
itching sores of lust until they bled. God took hold of that

man and turned him into probably the greatest theologian between the Apostle Paul and Calvin, whose writings have exerted a tremendous influence over evangelical Christianity throughout the centuries.

I was amazed at the courage of an Augustinian monk named Martin Luther who, when charged with heresy by the Church authorities for his writings on justification by faith, the priesthood of the believer and the absolute authority of the Scriptures, said, "What I have written, I have written. Here I stand; so help me God, I can do no other." As a result of that man's courage (through the grace of God in his life), the Protestant Reformation swept through Europe until it captured the heart of another man who loved God with all of his mind: John Calvin, who by the age of twenty-six had finished writing *The Institutes of the Christian Religion*.

I was thrilled to read how the Reformation spilled over into England, taking solid shape in the English Puritans— men and women who loved holiness with a passion, who recaptured a sense of the majesty and greatness of God. I learned how those same passions fueled Jonathan Edwards, acknowledged even by secular historians as America's greatest philosopher-theologian.

Then I read about William Carey rediscovering the impetus of world missions (apparently largely neglected by the Protestant Reformers) and launching the modern missionary movement so that in the last decade of the twentieth century, 20 to 40 million Christians around the world prayed regularly and strategically over the 10/40 Window,[5] preparing to tear down the last stronghold among the nations. I look at all that and I say, "Jesus was right—He will build His Church, and all the gates of hell will not prevail against it."

That's how I get my identity renewed—by being reminded that I am not just an individual; I am a functioning member of the Body of Christ, in the same "bloodline" as Augustine, Athanasius, Luther, Calvin and Edwards. Let the world laugh at me; let the world laugh at the Church; that's my identity—renewed by immersion in Church history.

Faith

The second thing that history gives us is faith. Thomas Oden says:

> If we are to understand the original meaning and value of our Christian faith, we must once again see it through the eyes of those who have had to struggle for it and maintain it at the risk of their lives. The martyrs, saints, and prophets of Christian history—more than recent riskless interpreters—can teach us the value of the classical Christian faith. Without their instruction our faith becomes a mere recollection, a bored nodding of the head, the source of an occasional laugh, or in emergency, an item to pawn.[6]

The more I begin to grasp the tremendous price that has been paid by the saints of God through the centuries for the privilege I have of preaching His Word every week and worshiping with the congregation that I am privileged to serve, the less likely I am to discard that faith in the face of trouble. I've also discovered that quite often, those who have done incredible acts of faith were not previously known to be courageous. In fact, one person I talked to in Poland said that he was somewhat of a coward—until he was thrown into a Communist prison. That gives me courage, because it says to me that the secret behind their faith is not *their* faithfulness but the faithfulness of Christ in times of difficulty. And my faith gets strengthened.

Wisdom

History is a source of wisdom as well. You remember that letter from the evangelical student? He wrote those words to the theologian Thomas Oden, who responded:

> The faddism of theology has not been accidental. . . .We
> have blithely assumed that in theology—just as in corn
> poppers, electric toothbrushes and automobile exhaust
> systems—new is good, newer is better, and newest is
> best. . . . New theologies appear every spring season with
> a wide assortment of "new moralities," "new hermeneu-
> tics," and . . . "revolutionary breakthroughs." On closer
> inspection, however, we will discover that all these views
> may be found in the writings of decades ago, except then
> with mercifully fewer pretensions and less hysteria.[7]

History teaches us to recognize old patterns, even though
they've been carefully disguised as "modern understanding."
The area of theology that relates to the battle of the sexes is a
perfect illustration of this. Radical feminist theology (and I
emphasize *radical* as opposed to the legitimate questions that
are being raised by godly women and men in the Church) is
founded on massive reinterpretation of the passages in Paul's
letters that deal with gender. It is portrayed to us as a
"brand-new" understanding. However, archeological discov-
eries (the Nag Hammadi texts, for example) reveal that very
similar, if not identical, reinterpretation of some of these
passages are to be found in gnosticism. Even more interesting is the fact that the gnostics didn't simply advocate equal-
ity between men and women; they promoted female goddess
worship, including serpent worship. And in some of the most
radical of current "Christian" feminist writings, they're calling for the same thing! It's not new—it's old, very old.

And we men have a few things to learn from history as
well. To my embarrassment, I have read passages from the
early Church fathers in which their interpretation of some of
Paul's statements on gender and their application to women
would make the most chauvinist male today cringe. (They
ought to make him weep and repent.) Both sexes need the
wisdom that comes from history because it enables us to say,
"*Deja vu*! I've seen this before. This isn't new; it's old."

C.S. Lewis suggested that for every new book we read, we should read an old book. Why? Because every age has its blind spot, and if we only read books written in our own age, we are reading with the same blind spot as the authors. But when we read a book written from another age, even though it has blind spots, they are different from ours, so they can speak to our blind spots. He summarized it beautifully in these words:

> Not, of course, that there is any magic about the past. People were no cleverer then than they are now; they made as many mistakes as we. But not the *same* mistakes. They will not flatter us in the errors we are already committing; and their own errors, being now open and palpable, will not endanger us. Two heads are better than one, not because either is infallible, but because they are unlikely to go wrong in the same direction.[8]

Renewal

Remembering the past is also a key to renewal. When I read of God's mighty works in renewing the Church throughout history, not only is my faith renewed, but so is my desire for God to do it again. Reading Arnold Dallimore's biography of George Whitefield was an eye-opening, heart-stirring and prayer-fueling look into what God did in eighteenth-century England through the preaching of Whitefield, John Wesley, John Cennick and Howel Harris, as well as through the hymns of Charles Wesley.

When I read Jonathan Edwards' memoirs of what happened on this side of the Atlantic during the first Great Awakening, even as Whitefield and Wesley were shaking all of England with Christ's power, when I read about the great revivals of the nineteenth century, about D.L. Moody's mission work, about the Student Volunteer Movement, about the Welsh revival, what does it do for me? It makes me stand and say, "LORD, I have heard of your fame; / I stand in awe of your deeds, O

LORD. / Renew them in our day, / in our time make them known; / in wrath remember mercy" (Habakkuk 3:2).

A grasp of history leads to a renewal not only of faith but of hope and desire. It gives me a whole new reason for being holy. There is a desire for holiness now in my life that goes beyond personal piety. It is an essential prerequisite to being a channel for revival. History also leads to renewal in methods, because the essence of the disease of modernity is a trust in human endeavor. And history shows us, more than anything else, that revival comes at the will of a sovereign God, as His people cry out to Him in prayer.

Dynamism

Finally, remembering the past is also the key to dynamism. In other words, a grasp of history also propels us to action, to do something about it. Let me give you a first-century illustration and a modern one. In Acts 4, Peter and John had been thrown into prison for preaching and for healing a lame man. They were charged not to preach in Jesus' name under threat of punishment. What did they do? They took recourse in history—sacred history recorded in their beloved Scriptures. They gathered together in a prayer meeting with minds that were totally shaped by biblical history. They went back a thousand years, when King David, in a similar position, with principalities and powers arrayed against him, wrote Psalm 2. Their history told them that it was all in vain—the opposition couldn't touch the anointed of God.

They then looked at their recent history, when Jesus Christ, the anointed of God, was also set upon by the rulers and authorities, and they didn't succeed either—they crucified Him, but God raised Him from the dead. And because of a keen historical sense, they reasoned, "What happened to David, what happened to Jesus, is what's going to happen to us—so let's get out there and do what we are supposed to do!" And they went out and preached in Jesus' name (see Acts 4:18, 23-31).

For a modern-day example of history as the source of dyna-mism, I refer once again to Thomas Oden, a seminary profes-sor who was at one time what evangelicals would term a rank liberal. He called himself a "movement" person; at the age of sixteen he was into the ecumenical movement, working for new world order. That was followed in succession by participa-tion in the anti-war movement, the early abortion-rights move-ment, the civil rights movement, the existential movement, the therapeutic movement and the parapsychology movement (the occult). He is now a devoted follower of Christ. What turned this man around? Here is his testimony:

> My irascible, endearing Jewish mentor, the late Will Herberg, straightforwardly told me . . . that I would re-main densely uneducated until I had read deeply in the classical Christian writers. . . . The very thinkers I once condemned scathingly as "conservative" I now find ever increasing in plausibility, depth, and wisdom. Once hesi-tant to trust anyone over thirty, now I hesitate to trust anyone under "three hundred." Once I thought it my sol-emn duty to read the *New York Times* almost every day; now seldom. Now it seems more important to know what Chrysostom taught about Galatians 2 or to hear Basil on the Holy Spirit rather than to know all the news that is not quite fit to print.[9]

Could it be that if we dared to read at least some of the great Christian classics, we might have a taste of Oden's ex-perience? I must admit, though, that some of them are very hard to read. If the prospect of tangling with these great gi-ants is too formidable to you, as it often has been for me, may I suggest that you read those modern authors whose own minds have been saturated and shaped by the Christian clas-sics? That's what makes Charles Colson, R.C. Sproul, C.S. Lewis, Os Guinness, John Piper, Eugene Peterson and J.I. Packer such significant writers. They have steeped their minds in the Christian classics.

Reading in General

I've focused on history so far for obvious reasons; let me conclude by discussing reading on a wider scale. In Philippians 4:8 we read these familiar words: "Finally, brothers, whatever is true, whatever is noble, whatever is right, whatever is pure, whatever is lovely, whatever is admirable—if anything is excellent or praiseworthy—think about such things." Often this verse has been applied to reading the Bible itself. But what people may not know is that this list of adjectives—true, noble, just, etc.—was not manufactured by Paul. It was already well known in the writings of Greek ethics and philosophy. Could it be that Paul was really saying that *anything in the world* that is true, noble, just, pure, etc., should be included in our reading and reflections? Paul understood that God's common grace gives wisdom even to unbelievers. And that applies specifically, I think, to literature.

Colson, in his book *The Body*, makes the observation that literature, because it can be read and reread, shared and passed down through time, has a lasting power to shape ideas.[10] Of course, when it comes to "taste" in books, we vary a lot. We prefer certain authors, certain sizes of print, a certain number of pages in a book. Some devour books of 900 pages; others don't like anything more than 90 pages. But I have discovered that, while there's a lot of room for variation, if we want to love God with our minds and resist modernity, there are three types of books that we all need to read.

The first type was driven home to me many years ago by a quote from Franz Kafka:

> If the book we are reading does not wake us as with a fist hammering on our skull, why then do we read it? So that it shall make us happy? Good God, we would also be happy if we had no books, and such books as make us happy we could, if need be, write ourselves. But what we must have are those books which come upon us like

> ill-fortune, and distress us deeply, like the death of one
> we love better than ourselves, like suicide. A book must
> be an ice axe to break the sea frozen inside us.[11]

We need to read books that break us. I can only share with
you my own experience of three books in particular that have
broken me along the way. The first one was Ronald Sider's
book *Rich Christians in an Age of Hunger*. It convinced me, per-
manently and unalterably, that the North American con-
sumer-oriented lifestyle is not just unwise; it is positively
sinful and disobedient. And it launched me, although I know
I still have a long way to go, on a journey toward a simplified
lifestyle in which my wife and I have learned to deliberately
live below our income level so that we can free up more of our
resources for the kingdom of God.

The second book that broke me was not just one book but a
group that I will term the "world Christian" literature, particularly Gordon Aeschliman's *The Hidden Half* and David Bryant's
In the Gap. These two books convinced me that every Christian
has a responsibility for the nations of the world to come to
know Jesus Christ. We either serve cross-culturally or we live
counterculturally in such a way as to partner with those who
serve cross-culturally in His vision for the lost; there is no other
alternative for a Christian who desires to be obedient.

The third book that broke me was Charles Colson's *The
Body*, for it showed me once again the absolutely critical importance of cultivating the virtue of courage—courage in my
own life and in the Church—so that we can be the kind of
Body that God intended the Church to be.

Books that break us, however, are not enough. Humpty
Dumpty can be pushed over the wall, but somebody has to put
him together again if he is to be of much use. So we also need
books that integrate us. Aleksandr Solzhenitsyn, himself a
master of literature, once asked the question, "Who will give
mankind one single system for reading its instruments . . . ?"[12]
His answer, presented during his 1970 Nobel lecture, is this:

> Literature . . . [has] the marvelous capacity of transmit-
> ting from one nation to another—despite differences in
> language, customs, and social structure—practical expe-
> rience, the harsh national experience of many decades,
> never tasted by the other nation. . . . Literature transmits
> condensed and irrefutable human experience in still an-
> other priceless way: from generation to generation. It
> thus becomes the living memory of a nation.[13]

And so good literature integrates us internationally. As
Katherine Paterson, an award-winning children's novelist,
puts it, "Really good books pull together for us a world that is
falling apart."[14] Books that break need to be combined with
books that integrate.

Four particular authors have immensely aided the integra-
tion process in my life. John Piper has integrated my theology more than anyone else. C.S. Lewis has integrated my
intellectual approach to Christianity. His book *Mere Christianity* is mentioned twice as often as any other in answer to
the question "Which Christian book, other than the Bible,
has impacted you more than anything else?"

Eugene Peterson has helped integrate my life vocationally.
He has taught me what it means to be a pastor. I have to be a
theologian who loves God and therefore disciplines his mind.
I have to be a poet who loves words and therefore exercises
his imagination. I have to be a pastor who loves people and
therefore listens to them carefully. Peterson has helped fashion and integrate my vocation. And the person who has
helped integrate my inner life, especially earlier in my life
when my children were young, is Gordon McDonald, with
his books *Ordering Your Private World*, *Rebuilding Your Broken
World* and *Living at High Noon*. The writings of these men
have helped integrate me theologically, intellectually, vocationally and internally.

In addition to books that break us and books that make us,
there are books that motivate us, that keep us going. Read
Peterson's insightful observation:

> Stanley Hauerwas argues, convincingly to me, that if we
> want to change our way of life, acquiring the right image
> is far more powerful than diligently exercising willpower.
> Willpower is a notoriously sputtery engine on which to
> rely for internal energy, but a right image silently and in-
> exorably pulls us into its field of reality, which is also a
> field of energy.[15]

Image motivates us in a way that sometimes willpower
cannot. I find that I increasingly need to collect and treasure
images that are going to keep me motivated. And the people
who have supplied these images? They include C.S. Lewis, in
his Chronicles of Narnia series; Peterson, in many of his
books, particularly *Reversed Thunder* and *Answering God*; Frederick Buechner, in *Truth, Allegory and Tragedy as the Gospel*;
and so many others that I have lost track.

So if we are going to love God with all our minds, not only
do we need to recover a sense of history and steep ourselves in
orthodoxy, but we also need to learn to read books that break
us, integrate us and motivate us. How do we do all this reading? There are a lot of practical considerations, objections and
obstacles to what I am proposing, to which we now turn.

Notes

1. Charles Colson, *The Body* (Dallas: Word, 1992), pp. 167-8.
2. Ibid., p. 167.
3. Thomas Oden, citing a letter from a student, in Os Guinness and John Seel, eds.,
   No God But God: Breaking with the Idols of Our Age (Chicago: Moody, 1992), p. 198.
4. Guinness and Seel, ibid., pp. 19-20.
5. The 10/40 Window refers to that region of the world between 10° and 40° north
   latitude and stretching from Africa on the west to Japan and the Philippines on
   the east. It has the largest concentration of "unreached people" and the poor.
6. Oden, in Guinness and Seel, p. 191.
7. Ibid., p. 195.
8. C.S. Lewis, *God in the Dock: Essays on Theology and Ethics* (Grand Rapids:
   Eerdmans, 1970), p. 202.
9. Guinness, citing Oden, *No God But God*, pp. 190-1.
10. Colson, *The Body*, passim.
11. Franz Kafka, as quoted by Eugene Peterson, *Working the Angles: The Shape of Pasto-
    ral Integrity* (Grand Rapids, MI: Eerdmans, 1990), pp. 132-3.

12. Aleksandr Solzhenitsyn, 1970 Nobel Lecture (trans. F.D. Reeve). September 24, 1999. March 13, 2003. Available from: <http://www.columbia.edu/cu/augustine/ arch/solzhenitsyn/nobel-lit1970.htm>.

13. Ibid.

14. From *Gates of Excellence: On Reading and Writing Books for Children* by Katherine Paterson, copyright © 1981 by Katherine Paterson, p. 17. Used by permission of Lodestar Books, an affiliate of Dutton Children's Books, a division of Penguin Young Readers Group, a member of Penguin Group (USA), Inc., 345 Hudson St., New York, NY 10014. All rights reserved.

15. Eugene Peterson, *Under the Unpredictable Plant* (Grand Rapids, MI: Eerdmans, 1992), p. 6.

8.

Objections, Obstacles, Costs

Many years ago, in the former Soviet Union, a ten-year-old girl named Irina sat in a dreary schoolroom, looking out the dirty window.[1] It was snowing outside—something that normally never happened in that little sea-side town of Odessa. Irina loved the snow, but as she kept watching it she became increasingly depressed, because she knew that by the time she went out to play, it all would have melted. Her mind was jerked back to the classroom by the raucous voice of the teacher. It was time for the regular in-doctrination in atheism.

As the teacher droned on, denying the existence of God in her by now familiar and well-rehearsed phrases, Irina thought to herself, *My parents only had to tell me once that there were no ghosts and then they forgot about it; why do the teachers have to keep telling us over and over again that there is no God? He must be real—and powerful, if they are so afraid of Him.*

And so Irina looked up to God and prayed her first prayer: *Listen, it's Your fault that I'm not able to play out in the snow. Will You let the snow continue?* God answered that prayer—it snowed for three days and three nights in Odessa! From that time on Irina began to talk to God regularly. She figured out for herself that the only kind of God she could believe in was a God who was all-powerful and also totally good.

The next significant event happened when she was four-teen years old, in the same classroom. While the teacher was out of the room, a kid from the back row threw a chestnut and hit an inkwell, splattering ink all over the floor. The irate teacher grilled the students one by one to find the culprit. Irina lied and said, "I was looking in my bag; I didn't see who it was." But when the teacher asked the boy next to Irina, he said, "I'm not gonna tell you."

Irina was struck by her cowardice and thought to herself, *I am becoming what they want me to be—a cowardly, spineless creature with no concept of honor, but ever obedient, one who considers a glib lie to be an act of heroism. I shall never lower myself like that again. If I must disobey in order to preserve my self-respect, I shall do so openly. Then my soul will remain my own; nobody will be able to manipulate me to suit themselves. I shall learn how to behave decently from books.*

Irina's mother, a teacher of literature, had saturated Irina's mind in the works of famous Russian authors, foremost among them being Dostoevsky and Tolstoy. And in their writings Irina began to discover a reflection of the God whom she had come to know and believe in, an all-powerful and all-wise God. But then came the inevitable onslaught of adolescence with its hormones and its doubts, and her beloved books were no longer helpful. Of course, Irina had no access to a Bible.

One day, as she was anguishing before God, Irina suddenly felt what was to become a familiar urge in her life, and she got up and wrote her first poem. She continued to exercise this gift for many years. At the age of twenty-three, Irina was given a Bible, but she couldn't read it—it was in an ancient dialect. In a month and a half she taught herself how to read that language, and then, for the first time in her life, she read the Word of God, and everything fell into place.

Irina went on to become a famous poet. As the KGB became aware of her poetry and the political climate hardened, she was arrested and sentenced to seven years of hard labor and seven years of internal exile. They tried their best, through cold and starvation, to break her spirit and kill her. But the resolve that was formed when she was fourteen, her beloved books, her Bible and her poetry kept Irina impervious. In the middle of KGB interrogations she would compose poetry in her mind and then awake at night to write it on scraps of paper. Eventually, because of pressure in the West, Irina was released. She came to the West and pursued a career as a writer and a poet.

What would have happened if, at the age of fourteen, Irina had not made that resolve to learn how to behave by reading good books? Irina's story, told in greater detail by Charles Colson in *The Body*, is a powerful illustration of the importance, as well as the critical long-term significance, of learning to love God with our minds.

Not many of us will ever be subjected to that kind of pressure—and we probably won't become celebrated poets, either!—but to love God with our minds, in the same way Irina did, is not an option for us. Everything we have discussed in previous chapters—resisting the encroachment of modernity, becoming theologians, sociologists, historians and people familiar with literature—all boils down to one basic commitment: We have to become readers. And while the details will differ from person to person in terms of individual preferences of authors, in the previous chapter I suggested three broad categories of books that we need to read: books that *break us* by revealing to us where modernity has affected us; books that *integrate us* vocationally, theologically, intellectually and personally; and books that *motivate us* by powerful, biblical images that pull us into their field of energy and reality.

I want to conclude our study of loving God with our minds with a very down-to-earth discussion of the practical objections, obstacles and costs—the things that get in the way of our becoming readers, and how we can resolve them and move ahead.

"It's Not for Laypeople"

The first objection is one that I hear quite often: "This is not for laypeople. It's OK for those who are intellectually inclined or for pastors and professors who do this as a profession. But we've got houses to maintain, businesses to run, children to raise. This isn't for us."

That argument may sound logical, but it doesn't square with the Scriptures. The disciples of Jesus were not exactly intellectuals. They were fishermen, tax collectors—as motley a crew as you could imagine—yet Jesus opened their minds to understand truth (see Luke 24:45). Paul, writing to laypeople, leaves no doubt as to their ability to learn the truth: "Then we will no longer be infants, tossed back and forth by the waves, and blown here and there by every wind of teaching and by the cunning and craftiness of men in their deceitful scheming" (Ephesians 4:14). And the author of Hebrews rebuked his readers, saying, "In fact, though by this time [most likely twenty years after they had first responded to the gospel] you ought to be teachers, you need someone to teach you the elementary truths of God's word all over again" (5:12). That was not written to specialists. It was written to ordinary Christians.

Throughout the centuries, the Lord Jesus Christ has been in the business of opening the minds of His followers. I read about a man named Carl Nelson, a senior executive for a large food manufacturer. He had over 1,500 books on the Christian classics in his personal library. He was so familiar with most of them that he was routinely asked to lecture at the nearby seminary, yet he had no theological training. In a previous chapter I mentioned a former colleague in ministry. He was twenty-eight years old, a supervisor with New Jersey Power and Light—about as "lay" as you can get. One day, in response to a challenge by a famous visiting apologist to devote his mind to God, he resolved, much like Irina, to do so. With no formal training in apologetics, philosophy or theol-

ogy, he went on to design and teach courses on all these subjects in university and church settings as well as mentor other
up-and-coming young apologists in many countries. I know
many other laymen and -women from all walks of life who
have learned to love God with all their minds. I think of one
who has been saturating his mind with the writings of a
twelfth-century monk named Bernard of Clairvaux. I know
others who have been digging into the writings of Jonathan
Edwards to shape their own theology and obedience. And I
know a mother with young children who waded her way
through the biography of George Whitefield—2 500-page
volumes! It can be done. It is for laypeople.

"It's Not My Gift"

However, you may say, "It's not my personality. You're a
thinker; I'm a feeler. Besides, it's not my gift. You are a
teacher. I don't have any gifts in teaching." It is certainly true
that differences in personality and gifting can make a difference in what we read, as well as how we process information,
relate to people and approach problems. But they have nothing to do with whether we are able to love God with our
minds. I know people who are at the opposite end of the gift
and personality spectrum from me, yet they have committed
and mobilized their minds to read, study, think, analyze and
teach. I learn a lot from them, precisely because of the difference in their perspectives.

"I'm Too Old"

Some may say, "I'm too old; it's too late for me to start loving God with my mind." Don't believe it! Howard Hendricks,
a veteran teacher and an older saint who hasn't stopped loving
God with his mind, has observed that many older people avoid
learning on the theory that "you can't teach an old dog new
tricks." With his typically wry sense of humor, Hendricks says

that while that theory may apply to dogs, and while it may apply to teaching tricks, it has nothing to do with people! Once they accept that they have the capacity to love God with their minds, older people can be excellent learners.

"I'm Too Young"

How about "I'm too young"—the opposite end of the spectrum? If you're old enough to watch television, you're old enough to have been infected thoroughly with the disease of modernity, and you cannot afford to put off learning to love God with your mind.

Don't underestimate the capacity of young minds to learn. At one conference I went to in England, one of the delegates was seventeen years old. He spoke five languages: Arabic, Armenian, Swedish, English and French. And on the last day of the conference he was following me everywhere, constantly asking questions. He was that eager to learn, and he did.

While I was on a speaking assignment in Colombia, my interpreter told me that the average teenager from Colombia is not much different than the average teen from North America, except for one thing: The Colombian students are quite familiar with the writings of Plato and Aristotle. They're into philosophy already. Irina was only fourteen when she set her mind to learn how to behave by reading Dostoevsky and Tolstoy. It can be done. Don't underestimate your capacity.

"I Don't Have Time"

Finally, you may agree with the importance of loving God with our minds, but you insist, "I don't have enough time to do it." Paul addresses that in Ephesians 5:15-17: "Be very careful, then, how you live—not as unwise but as wise, making the most of every opportunity, because the days are evil. Therefore do not be foolish, but understand what the Lord's will is." The phrase translated "making the most of every opportunity" literally means "redeem [buy up] the time." It was marketplace language, used when you redeemed someone from slavery by paying the price of bondage. Paul uses that graphic word picture to drive home to us the fact that our time has been enslaved by the society in which we live. He says to get it back. Redeem the time. Buy up the opportunity. Pay whatever it costs to set your time free so that you can become wise people. Why? Because the days are evil, and you need to understand what the will of the Lord is.

The real danger with all of these objections—none of which are valid in any final or determinative sense—is that they tend to cover up the real culprits, the obstacles that get in our way. So let me move from these spurious objections to the three key obstacles.

Obstacle #1: Laziness

The first—and I'm afraid we have to deal with it—is laziness. Scott Peck, in his book *The Road Less Traveled*, asks this question: "Since the path of spiritual growth, albeit difficult, is open to all, why do so few choose to travel it?" His answer, based on fifteen years of honest observation of himself and his clients, is, "It is our laziness . . . that causes us ...to stay at the comfortable, easy rung where we now are or even to descend to less and less demanding forms of existence."[2]

He tells an interesting, and for me unforgettable, story about a brilliant young woman who used to come to him for therapy. She was caught in a web of unhealthy relationships in which she was constantly manipulated by others. Through coaching and therapy, she got to the point where she could analyze one particular relationship, learn to respond to it properly and experience freedom for the first time in her life. She came to Peck's office one day, her eyes bright with excitement, and shared this victory. But when Peck pointed out how, by doing the same kind of analysis of all her other relationships, she could get greater and greater freedom, she responded, "But that means I have to think all the time! I didn't come here to make my life more difficult; I just want to be able to relax and enjoy myself!" Then she stormed out of the therapy session and never came back.[3]

Laziness is an ever-present challenge, and Scripture warns us very clearly about it. The writer of Hebrews, in the same context as the verse that says, "Though by this time you ought to be teachers" (5:12), says, "We want each of you to show this same diligence to the very end, in order to make your hope sure. We do not want you to become lazy, but to imitate those who through faith and patience inherit what has been promised" (6:11-12). In the context of one of the most serious (if not the most serious) warnings in the entire Bible, he identifies laziness as the core problem.

Obstacle #2: Amusement

A second obstacle is this activity we term amusement. Several years ago, I was quite surprised to learn that the root of this word, *muse*, is Latin for "think," while the prefix *a-* simply means "not." So amusement is *unthinking* activity.

This could explain why our North American society has the maximum amount of leisure time and opportunities for amusement yet is one of the most tired, fatigued and frazzled societies we know. As the title of Neil Postman's book puts it, we are "amusing ourselves to death." While there are many sources for this amusement that passes off for refreshment and recreation, the number one culprit is television.[4]

Four Arguments for the Complete Elimination of Television by Jerry Mander is a book that I would certainly categorize as one that "breaks" us. He noted that many people referred to the "hypnotic effect" of TV, so he consulted with psychologists specializing in hypnosis, who verified this popular view. The speed and volume of images that television produces overwhelm one's thinking processes so that the information presented bypasses the critical mind.[5]

But you might say, "I find it relaxes me so much." Mander's research, however, calls into question TV's "relaxing" effects. If you want to relax and calm your mind, you need to cease thinking. Television does not allow that to happen, but it also does not stimulate and exercise the mind in a way that causes healthy reflection and contemplation. With so many images pouring into it from the "one-eyed monster," the mind never gets to rest.[6]

It certainly looks like Postman is right. We *are* "amusing ourselves to death."

Obstacle #3: Avoidance

The third obstacle is avoidance of community, and it is rooted in either pride or fear or both. We don't take time to talk to other people from whom we can learn. Older people and those who have suffered are a tremendous source of wisdom for the development of the mind. Leighton Ford used to say, "If you really want to know wisdom, ask people who have suffered much and who have emerged with their faith intact at the end of the suffering." Avoidance of community also keeps us isolated from others who can hold us accountable in this area. Are you reading? Why not? *What* are you reading? How are you using what you're reading? We need to give others the privilege and responsibility to ask us questions like that.

Counting the Cost

These spurious objections and the three primary obstacles behind them (and there may be others) are important for us to learn about, but what you may need at this point is motivation. We could talk about the benefits of loving God with all our minds, but sometimes, when things are going relatively well, the benefits of doing something are not enough to motivate us. The awesome costs of not doing them, however, may. Let's take a look at the costs of refusing to love God with all our minds.

Cost #1: Mental Flabbiness

The first cost of doing nothing is mental flabbiness, which makes us more and more vulnerable to the infection of modernity—or any other prevailing philosophy. Eventually, we can even lose the ability to think for ourselves. We've seen its most extreme forms in the past few decades with Jim Jones and his followers in Guyana, as well as David Koresh and the Branch Davidian chaos in Waco, Texas. But in its less virulent form, this kind of thing is happening every day. Mental flabbiness makes us go from one extreme to another, victims of the latest newsletter, the latest article in the *New York Times*, or—ironically—the latest best-selling book!

Cost #2: Doubt

The second cost of not loving God with all our minds is doubt. Os Guinness, in his book *God in the Dark*, shares this insight:

> To think and not understand is one problem; not to think and have no chance of understanding is a greater one. A keen mind will rarely remain idle and satisfied. If the faith by which it lives does not allow it room to move, the mind is apt to exact its own revenge. A good mind denied by bad faith will self-destruct with insecurity, guilt, fanaticism, or doubt.[7]

Guiness is warning that if you keep on saying, "I just believe, that's all," but never ask yourself why, you never stretch your mind. Eventually, a good mind denied by bad faith will rebel—sometimes with guilt, sometimes with fanaticism, sometimes with doubt. And that kind of doubt, if left unchecked, will eventually descend into skepticism and maybe even apostasy.

Cost #3: Legalism

A third cost of an unthinking mind is that it is much more prone to legalism and related relational problems. Gordon

MacDonald, in his book *Ordering Your Private World*, makes the observation that many believers "appear to be afraid to think." They may gather facts and accumulate lists of pat answers, but when it comes to dealing with complex issues that have no simple solutions, they shy away from the challenge. Such a refusal to use one's God-given intellectual capacity, MacDonald says, results in "mediocrity in personal living and mental activity."[8]

And mediocrity in personal living and mental activity in a Christian setting almost always leads to legalism, because you want every concept neatly packaged, every question wrapped up in an easy-to-swallow-and-digest pill, with no troubling loose ends. If you challenge an individual like that, he is apt to respond with anger, denial, counteraccusations or a sullen withdrawal—but seldom with an open-minded engagement of a viewpoint that differs from his own.

Cost #4: A Bankrupt Faith

A fourth cost of not using our minds is a bankruptcy in times of suffering. We don't know what lies ahead for us, but when suffering comes, we may find that we have nothing to keep us going. Irina survived the concentration camps in Siberia because of the resolve she made at the age of fourteen. I read about Katherine Koob, one of the sixty-seven hostages in Iran in the 1970s. She survived remarkably and even helped other people; she was a real source of inspiration. When asked afterwards what her secret was, she said that it was her years of reading and the commitment of that reading, especially of Scripture, to memory.[9] In her mind was an incredible storehouse of truth that she could draw upon to sustain herself, to inspire others and to maintain resolve in a time of difficulty.

Cost #5: Tongue-Tied Evangelism

A fifth cost of not loving God with our minds is that we become totally tongue-tied in evangelism. I often run into peo-

ple who say, "Pastor, I met so-and-so, who is a Hindu (or a
New Ager, or an evolutionist). How should I witness to
him?" There is no way I can, in a short conversation, explain
how to communicate across worldviews that are so vastly different! It is not an easy formula that you learn in ten minutes. It comes from a lifetime of learning how to communicate across worldviews by studying, putting what you
learn into practice, doing an honest postmortem on the effort, refining and trying again—and keeping this up for the
rest of your life. The resources are there; the opportunities
are there. The only thing that keeps us from availing ourselves of them are the obstacles of laziness, amusement and
avoidance. And yet what did Peter say? "Prepare your minds
for action. . . . Always be prepared to give an answer to everyone who asks you to give the reason for the hope that you
have" (1 Peter 1:13; 3:15). And remember, he was writing to
a suffering church.

Cost #6: Profane and Cliché-Ridden Speech

A sixth cost of an unthinking mind (and this one may surprise you) is profane and cliché-ridden speech, which, more
often than we think, comes from a poor mind, not a bad
heart. When someone mentions profanity, we usually think
immediately of all the forbidden four-letter words. But if you
think about it, many of them are just shorthand for other
words that are perfectly appropriate in the English language.
What makes them profane is that they are used in the wrong
place. The word *profane* comes from the Latin *profanum*,
which has been variously translated "across the threshold" or
"outside the temple." That which is sacred is being used in a
common fashion, and in that light, a lot of us who never
swear are guilty of profanity.

I see it most often in prayer. I catch it every now and then
in my own prayers. We often use the names and titles of God
almost as a punctuation mark while we are thinking what to

say next. Some people say "Lord" six or seven times in every sentence. An Old Testament scribe wouldn't even look up when he was writing the name *Yahweh*. It was written without vowels (Hebrew scholars refer to it as the *tetragrammaton*) so that people wouldn't even pronounce the name. And we unthinkingly toss in seven or eight of them in a single sentence. Profanity! That's what it really is.

Often, when praying for someone in need, you may hear people say, "Lord, be with him in a very real way. Be with this missionary in a very special way." Think about that. What does it mean to ask God to be with someone "in a very real way" or "in a very special way"? Change the imagery for a minute. You and your spouse are going out for dinner and you're leaving your two children with a babysitter. How often do you say to the babysitter, "Now be with my children in a very real way. Be with my children in a very special way"? No, you tell them, "Don't forget, at eight o'clock Susie has to get her medicine," or "I'm expecting a call at 9:30, so be sure you take a message," or "They need to be in bed by ten." You give them specific instructions.[10]

But when we pray to God, it's, "Lord, be with them in a very special way. Be with them in a very real way. Bless them. Good night." A lot of this cliché-ridden speech comes not because our hearts are wrong but because our minds have not been exercised. There's no storehouse of visual imagery, phraseology or terms of expression that you acquire from exercising your mind in reading.

And my question simply is this: For the luxury of hiding behind the five objections, or the convenience of refusing to overcome the three obstacles listed above, is this the cost that you want to pay—being mentally flabby, full of doubt, legalistic, close-minded, bankrupt in suffering, tongue-tied in evangelism and profane and cliché-ridden in speech? I don't, and I hope you don't either.

Suggestions for Reading

If you do decide, for these and other reasons, to start reading (or continue reading, if you already are), how do you read a book? It's not enough to read if you can't retain and recall what you read. Jesus said that the good soil in the parable of the sower is the true and noble heart that retains what it hears and by perseverance brings fruit (see Matthew 13:23). So I'd like to give a few suggestions on how to do that.

1. *Make a brief summary of every chapter* as you read. It doesn't take very long—just compile the key points of the chapter that have touched you. When I do this, I find that later I can review a 300-page book in about 30 minutes, just by reading the chapter summaries.

2. Take some of the most powerful passages of the book and *write them in your journal*. If you don't have a journal, start one for this very reason. I initially found it helpful to divide my journal into four major categories of my life: personal (what happens in my inner life), prayer (my life of communion with God), family (my marriage and my children) and ministry (preaching, teaching, counseling, etc.). Every time I come across something that is really powerful, whether it breaks me, integrates me or motivates me, I take some time to jot it in the appropriate section of my journal. Of course, nowadays, with the ubiquitous computer and database programs that many of us use all the time, it is that much easier to keep track of such material and index it for easy retrieval. And that's what I often do.

3. *Review the journal entries on a regular basis*. I have found four profitable ways to review journal entries. First, I use them regularly in my meditation and in my prayer time. Some days when the juices aren't flowing, I open my journal and just start reading. Often on Sunday mornings I used to read the section on ministry. Second, I use them in writing letters to missionaries and friends, sharing with them the

things that I have learned. Third, I use them in teaching—in small groups, preaching and other settings. Fourth, some of the most powerful passages that I don't want to forget I have posted in my Bible and in various places in my study—at eye level, so I see them on a regular basis.

4. Redeem time by *making appointments with the author* you are reading. You make appointments with your doctor, dentist, even your plumber—and you usually keep them. Write in at least one appointment a week with the author you are reading, and you will find that the reading gets done.

The endnotes in each chapter of this book refer to several books and authors who have radically affected my life. You may want to start with one of those. Obviously, I can only suggest books that I have read myself, so the list is very subjective. But it's a place to get started.

Irina had absolutely no idea when she started reading at the age of fourteen what was ahead of her. None of us has any idea of what lies ahead of us. We don't have any control over the end results, but we do have a lot of control over what we do now to prepare for the unknown future.

Notes

1. Paraphrased story from Charles Colson, *The Body* (Dallas: Word, 1992), pp. 75-81.
2. M. Scott Peck, *The Road Less Traveled* (New York: Simon & Schuster, 1980), pp. 297, 301.
3. Ibid., p. 303.
4. Neil Postman, *Amusing Ourselves to Death* (New York: Viking, 1985), passim.
5. Jerry Mander, *Four Arguments for the Elimination of Television* (New York: William Morrow, 1978), passim.
6. Ibid.
7. Os Guinness, *God in the Dark: The Assurance of Faith Beyond a Shadow of Doubt* (Wheaton, IL: Crossway, 1996), p. 167.
8. Gordon MacDonald, *Ordering Your Private World* (Nashville: Thomas Nelson, 1985), p. 97.
9. Katherine Koob, *Guest of the Revolution* (Nashville: Thomas Nelson, 1984), passim.
10. I use this same illustration to make a different point in my book on the Psalms, *The Conquest of Inner Space: Learning the Language of Prayer* (Toronto: Scarlet Cord Press, 2003).

9.

With All Your Strength

When I was in the middle of preaching the sermon series from which this book was derived, I mentioned at a church staff meeting that I had finished preaching on loving God with all your heart and mind, so I planned to move on to the next part of Jesus' statement: loving your neighbor as yourself. I was immediately taken aback by another staff member's comment: "You've forgotten something. What about loving God with all your strength?"

I hadn't really planned to preach a whole sermon on that, because I didn't know what there was to say. To do anything with all your strength simply means to give it all you've got. Therefore, loving God with all your strength simply means taking all the things that we learned about loving God with all our hearts and minds and giving it everything we've got. End of sermon.

But his question made me think back to how this series of messages got started. I had been reading Jesus' declaration that the two greatest commandments are loving God and loving your neighbor when I was struck by the verse that says, "All the Law and the Prophets hang on these two commandments" (Matthew 22:40). The Holy Spirit had arrested me with the force of Jesus' words in a way that I'd known only on a few occasions.

And when the Lord asked me, "Have you given these two commandments the attention that they deserve?" I had to admit that my answer was no. That's how these messages came about.

The staff member's question made me realize that if I had been guilty of not giving enough attention to these two commandments, perhaps I was still guilty of not giving enough attention to the different aspects of the commandments. And so I knew that I had to do some more thinking about what it meant to love God with all our strength.

As I meditated on this, God in His mercy directed me to a portion of Scripture that serves as a framework for my further reflections on loving God with all our strength. I had not realized till this point that there is only one individual in the whole Bible about whom it is explicitly said that he turned to God with all of his heart, mind and strength: "Neither before nor after Josiah was there a king like him who turned to the LORD as he did—with all his heart and with all his soul and with all his strength, in accordance with all the Law of Moses" (2 Kings 23:25).

When I looked at the incidents surrounding God's commendation of Josiah, I realized that, when it comes to loving God with all our strength, the focus of Scripture is not so much on the methodology (give it everything you've got) as on the motivation. What is it that motivates us to "give it everything we've got"—to love God with all our hearts and minds?

First, some historical background. Josiah was a king of Judah—the southern kingdom. He was king over Judah about 200 years after Israel, the northern kingdom, had gone into exile, conquered and deported by the Assyrian king Sennacherib. At the age of twenty-six, in the eighteenth year of his reign, Josiah decided to renovate the temple of God, which had fallen into disrepair, if not disuse.

Warning of Judgment

When the workmen got going, Hilkiah, the high priest, found a copy of the Book of the Law—either Deuteronomy or

the first five books of the Bible, from Genesis through Deuteronomy. He gave it to the king's secretary, who read the whole
book to the king. (Reading at a normal speed, this would take
roughly three hours for Deuteronomy, or twelve hours for all
five books.) As the king listened, here's what happened:

> When the king heard the words of the Book of the Law,
> he tore his robes. He gave these orders to Hilkiah the
> priest, Ahikam son of Shaphan, Acbor son of Micaiah,
> Shaphan the secretary and Asaiah the king's attendant:
> "Go and inquire of the LORD for me and for the people
> and for all Judah about what is written in this book that
> has been found. Great is the LORD's anger that burns
> against us because our fathers have not obeyed the words
> of this book; they have not acted in accordance with all
> that is written there concerning us." (22:11-13)

Josiah was motivated to love God with all of his strength
because he took seriously the warning of impending judgment. They and their forefathers had treated the worship of
God casually and not listened to the Word of God about the
proper way to worship.

It is no different when we look at the New Testament, for it
too contains serious warnings against forsaking God. In Hebrews we find five of the most awesome warnings in the New
Testament (directed to professing believers) woven throughout the book and connected with some of its greatest promises.
Here they are:

> We must pay more careful attention, therefore, to what
> we have heard, so that we do not drift away. For if the
> message spoken by angels was binding, and every viola-
> tion and disobedience received its just punishment, how
> shall we escape if we ignore such a great salvation?
> (2:1-3)

> See to it, brothers, that none of you has a sinful, unbeliev-
> ing heart that turns away from the living God. (3:12)

It is impossible for those who have once been enlightened, who have tasted the heavenly gift, who have shared in the Holy Spirit, who have tasted the goodness of the word of God and the powers of the coming age, if they fall away, to be brought back to repentance, because to their loss they are crucifying the Son of God all over again and subjecting him to public disgrace. (6:4-6)

If we deliberately keep on sinning after we have received the knowledge of the truth, no sacrifice for sins is left, but only a fearful expectation of judgment and of raging fire that will consume the enemies of God. (10:26-27)

See to it that you do not refuse him who speaks. If they did not escape when they refused him who warned them on earth, how much less will we, if we turn away from him who warns us from heaven? (12:25)

What's the relevance of these five warnings to loving God with all our hearts, souls, minds and strength? Simply this: Hebrews was written to convince us that we can and therefore should draw near to God, enter the most holy place and learn to hear God speak so that we can speak to Him and worship Him—which, of course, is what loving God is all about. And this incredible privilege of access to the most holy God is rooted in the infinite superiority of Jesus over the Old Testament "greats" (the angels, the prophets, Moses, Aaron, Joshua) and the infinite superiority of His work as our High Priest based on an infinitely superior offering (His own blood) in an infinitely superior tabernacle (in heaven, not on earth).

In that context, the last warning from the author of Hebrews is, "Do not refuse him who speaks" (12:25). He is referring to the tragic episode in Exodus when God spoke from Mount Sinai. The Israelites shut up their ears and said, "We can't bear to hear God speak. Moses, you go listen to God and come back and tell us what He said. We'll be satisfied with that" (see Exodus 20:19). And a few verses earlier, he had also exhorted his readers not to be "profane" like Esau, who sold his birthright for a single meal.

The writer of Hebrews is saying that all of us have an incredible privilege of direct access to God the Father and of hearing His voice (our birthright), and we should not refuse to do it. To do so is to profane our birthright—to treat it as commonplace. Therefore, we should never say, "Pastor, you're good at listening to God; come and preach to us and we'll listen to you." I'm glad when people show up to hear me preach, but I have failed if I don't point them to Christ.

Don't say, "You do it!" Don't refuse Him who speaks from heaven. To the extent that we allow the seriousness of these warnings to grip our hearts because of the greatness of the privilege, to that extent will we learn to love God with all our strength, as well as with our hearts and minds.

That was the first thing that gripped Josiah—warning of impending judgment. This has some practical implications for our private as well as our corporate lives, but because Hebrews 12 ends with an invitation to corporate worship, let's look at a few corporate implications, just to stimulate your thinking.

It means, first of all, that when you come to a worship service you should come prepared to hear God speak. That means you're going to pay attention to everything that goes on. He doesn't just speak when someone preaches; He speaks through a line in a hymn or through a testimony, so come prepared to listen throughout the service. It also means you come prepared to fully enter into the privilege of joyful worship with brothers and sisters. There are some dimensions of corporate worship that you simply cannot reproduce in private worship at home or out in "nature."

It means that you don't casually saunter into a service twenty or thirty minutes after it has started, just to listen to the sermon. It also means that you don't waste your time and energy on late Saturday night "bashes" because of which you can barely stay awake on Sunday morning.

These are just some practical implications of taking these warnings seriously because of the incredible greatness of the privilege that is before us. And the more that the reality of these warnings sinks in, the more we will love God with all our strength.

A **Kairos** Moment

When Josiah heard the words of impending judgment from the Book of the Law, he sent his people to a prophetess by the name of Huldah to find out the full import of what had been read to him from God's law. She sent them back with this message to Josiah:

> Tell the king of Judah, who sent you to inquire of the LORD, "This is what the LORD, the God of Israel, says concerning the words you heard: Because your heart was responsive and you humbled yourself before the LORD when you heard what I have spoken against this place and its people, that they would become accursed and laid waste, and because you tore your robes and wept in my presence, I have heard you, declares the LORD. Therefore I will gather you to your fathers, and you will be buried in peace. Your eyes will not see all the disaster I am going to bring on this place." (2 Kings 22:18-20)

You can almost imagine Josiah saying, "Whew—saved by the bell! Even though God is going to destroy the people, at least I'm OK." But Josiah didn't do that! And when we look at what he did and why he did it, we learn the second thing that motivated Josiah:

> Then the king called together all the elders of Judah and Jerusalem. He went up to the temple of the LORD with the men of Judah, the people of Jerusalem, the priests and the prophets—all the people from the least to the greatest. He read in their hearing all the words of the Book of the Covenant, which had been found in the temple of the LORD.

> The king stood by the pillar and renewed the covenant in
> the presence of the LORD—to follow the LORD and keep
> his commands, regulations and decrees with all his heart
> and all his soul, thus confirming the words of the covenant
> written in this book. Then all the people pledged them-
> selves to the covenant. (23:1-3)

Why did he do that? Because he was a godly man, and he
knew from the history of his own people that the welfare of
the people was often wrapped up in the welfare of the king.
Even though God had declared His intention to destroy the
people, Josiah knew that if he exercised his authority as king
and availed himself of this opportunity to influence the people and institute national reform, maybe God in His mercy
would relent and have mercy on the entire nation.

Josiah was motivated not only by the solemnity of the impending judgment but also by the possibility that he might
take advantage of what is known as a *kairos* moment in his
life. This was a moment to act, and if he missed it, it might
never come again. New Testament Greek has two different
words for time: *chronos* and *kairos*. *Chronos* is quantity of time.
It's the kind of time we mean when we say something like,
"How much more *time* before this service is over?" That can
be answered with a specific quantity of time, such as
twenty-five minutes.

But if a stockbroker says to you, "I've been watching the
market, and it's getting ready to take off; this is the *time* to
buy," that's *kairos* time. That's time that is not measured in
quantity but is seen qualitatively as an opportunity—a moment to act, and if you don't, it's gone forever. The New Testament emphasizes *kairos*, not *chronos*. Notice the use of the
word *time* in these verses—and they are all in the implied or
explicit context of loving God with our hearts:

- Mark 1:15: " 'The *time* has come,' he said. 'The kingdom of God is near. Repent and believe the good
  news!' " Of course, the kingdom of God was con-

cretely present in the person of Jesus Christ. Christ is near; it is the opportunity for contact with Jesus.

- Luke 19:44: "They will dash you [speaking of the city of Jerusalem] to the ground, you and the children within your walls. They will not leave one stone on another, because you did not recognize the *time* of God's coming to you." They had prayed for this Messiah for hundreds of years—and here was God Almighty in the flesh. They could touch Him, talk to Him, eat with Him, sit at His feet, worship Him and drink in His beauty—and they crucified Him instead. He wept over Jerusalem and said, "You did not know the time of My coming. You missed your opportunity for intimacy with God."

- Romans 13:11: "And do this, understanding the present *time*. The hour has come for you to wake up from your slumber, because our salvation is nearer now than when we first believed." Every moment is a *kairos* moment for the Christian. This verse has incredible historical significance, because way back in the fifth century, God used it to turn around a debauched, decadent man by the name of Augustine, who learned to love God with a legendary passion.

- First Corinthians 7:29: "What I mean, brothers, is that the *time* is short. From now on those who have wives should live as if they had none." What did Paul mean by that? He was answering questions that the Corinthians had about singlehood and marriage, but he also wanted to make it clear that there was something more important than all that; as verse 31 says, "this world in its present form is passing away." Everything in this world is temporal— even marriage—but the time to act is right now, whether you are married or single. Don't let that stop you from taking hold of the *kairos* moments of your life.

- Revelation 1:3: "Blessed is the one who reads the words of this prophecy, and blessed are those who hear it and take to heart what is written in it, because the *time* is near." The word translated "read" means to "read aloud." Why was it important to read aloud the Word of God? Reading the Word aloud suggests that the Word is intended to be a voice—a voice that propels us into the throne room, where Jesus Christ is seated with God the Father. We can hear Him speak to us in that living voice, and we can speak back to Him, ascribing glory, honor, power and majesty to Him forever and ever. Take heed to His voice, because the time is near.

These verses have the same message as the book of Hebrews, but the emphasis is different. Instead of serious warnings, we are called to give God everything to avoid missing the *kairos* moment. I am reminded of Brutus' words in Shakespeare's *Julius Caesar*:

> There is a tide in the affairs of men
>   Which, if taken at the flood, leads on to fortune;
> Omitted, all the voyage of their life
>   Is bound in shallows and miseries.
> On such a full sea are we now afloat.
>   We must take the current where it serves,
> Or lose our ventures.[1]

My mind goes back to a young dentist at a seminar in India. He was in the first group of people whom a colleague and I had the privilege of training in a seminar on apologetics and spiritual disciplines that we would go on to teach in various parts of the world over the next several years. At the end of the first session, he stood up, looked at all the delegates and said, "Do you know what God has done for us? This is the first time this material is being taught anywhere. From a country of 800 million people, we thirty-seven people have been given this opportunity. What are you going to do with it?"

Is it any wonder that this man turned out to be our star trainee and is now teaching other people? There was a tide in the affairs of his life that he took at the flood. And yet I cannot help but think of many others who omitted it; who knows what kinds of shallows and miseries their lives are bogged down in today?

Could this be what the Holy Spirit is saying to you? Could it be that the church you belong to, the ministries you perform, the Sunday school class you attend, even this book on loving God with all you've got, are *kairos* moments in your life? The tide is at flood, ready for you. Will you ride the wave? What if you miss it?

The Reality of Battle

The extent to which the warnings of Hebrews grip our hearts is the extent to which we will give God all our strength. So too the extent to which the horror of missing our *kairos* moment grips our heart is the extent to which we will give Him all our strength.

But how is that actually worked out? What did it mean for Josiah? He was motivated by these two things, so he instituted a covenant renewal. But then he went even further. And in that we will find the third element that motivates us.

Josiah went on to institute a radical cleansing of the entire country, ridding it of idols and anything else that reminded the people of the worship of pagan gods—particularly Molech, that god of the abominable child sacrifice. Notice the verbs that the Holy Spirit used to describe Josiah's actions:

> He took the Asherah pole from the temple of the LORD
> to the Kidron Valley outside Jerusalem and *burned* it

there. He *ground* it to powder and *scattered* the dust over the graves of the common people. . . .

He *pulled* down the altars the kings of Judah had erected on the roof near the upper room of Ahaz, and the altars Manasseh had built in the two courts of the temple of the LORD. He removed them from there, *smashed* them to pieces and *threw* the rubble into the Kidron Valley. . . . Josiah *smashed* the sacred stones and *cut* down the Asherah poles and *covered* the sites with human bones [a sign of desecration].

Even the altar at Bethel, the high place made by Jeroboam son of Nebat, who had caused Israel to sin—even that altar and high place he *demolished*. He *burned* the high place and *ground* it to powder, and *burned* the Asherah pole also. (2 Kings 23:6, 12, 14-15)

I love the words that begin verse 16 of that same chapter: "Then Josiah looked around. . . ." He wanted to make sure there wasn't anything he'd forgotten! But why did he bother? After all, he had led the people in a magnificent covenant-renewal ceremony. Those idols, poles and altars could have made good museum pieces. Why destroy them? We get a clue in verse 24:

Furthermore, Josiah got rid of the mediums and spiritists, the household gods, the idols and all the other detestable things seen in Judah and Jerusalem. This he did to fulfill the requirements of the law written in the book that Hilkiah the priest had discovered in the temple of the LORD.

The mediums and spiritists are always the last to go; they hang on right to the end. And Josiah was wise enough to realize that behind all of the desecration, the disrepair of the temple and the ignorance of the true God was the activity of an enemy who never quits. That's the third thing that motivates us to love God with all our strength: the reality of battle with an unrelenting and crafty opponent.

Notice how the book of Ephesians begins with blessing: "Praise be to the God and Father of our Lord Jesus Christ, who has *blessed us in the heavenly realms* with every spiritual blessing in Christ" (1:3). In the next chapter there is the blessing of our exaltation with Christ: "And God raised us up with Christ and *seated us with him in the heavenly realms*" (2:6). But in chapter 6, it's warfare: "For our struggle is not against flesh and blood, but against the rulers, against the authorities, against the powers of this dark world and against the *spiritual forces of evil in the heavenly realms*" (6:12). The sphere of blessing and the place of exaltation—"the heavenly realms"—is also the place of warfare.

As I was working on the original sermon behind this chapter, I got a call from someone who used to attend my church but had not been coming for a long time. This person was suffering a lot, partly because of circumstances beyond his control and partly because of his own sinfulness. This person mentioned that he had happened to drop in for a service recently. I said, "Well, does that mean that you might consider coming back?"

"Oh, no," he responded. "I felt such an incredible oppression in that church, I had to get out as quickly as I could."

I couldn't leave a statement like that alone, so I said to him, "I need some clarification. There are two ways in which you can feel oppression in a place. People who are close to God feel oppression when they go to a place where demonic forces are very evidently at work. But it works the other way around too. People who are not close to God can feel a tremendous oppression where the Spirit of God is present in power. Holiness is not always pleasant. Not when we are walking disobediently."

I will never forget his answer; he said, "Both." And he added, "There is a tremendous warfare going on in your church. There are a lot of people who are determined to love God with all their hearts, seek His face and pray. And there are a lot of peo-

ple who have dragged a lot of garbage into that church. I don't
know who the people are. I just know there's warfare."

Then he said, "Well, how do you react to that?"

I said, "Frankly, I'm not particularly disturbed; I'm even
glad. When I started my ministry here, I read a statement by
Howard Hendricks in *Leadership* magazine to the effect that
if you are moving your church in the right direction, you can
be assured of two things: God's presence and power, but also
Satan's activity."

As we move closer to the end of history, I think that the
lines will be drawn a lot more clearly. The middle ground will
be shrinking. The fence is going to get so thin that it's going
to be incredibly uncomfortable to remain seated on it. And
we're going to have to come down on one side or the other.
It's high time we saw ourselves as soldiers in a battle.

Years ago a member of my congregation wrote me a letter
on this same issue. With her permission, I'd like to quote a
paragraph from it: "Thanks for your sermon on courage. My
heartstrings were drawn to follow. It seems to me that until
we begin to see the Church of Jesus Christ, not as a Sunday
school picnic, but as a cause that we join as soldiers who conquer, we will not have the necessary ingredients to make it."

Understanding that we are in a battle can really improve our
perspective. I once counseled someone who felt ripped off and
constricted by his Christianity and blamed his Christianity for
his singleness. I told him that I thought that a correct concept
of Christianity had been withheld from him at his conversion.
He had come to be relieved of his problems; apparently he did-
n't know that he was joining an army and a cause.

It has been a great help to me personally to see myself as a
soldier. I tend to stop expecting to be pampered; instead of
looking around at what I've missed, it helps me focus on the
cause and what I can contribute. Don't get me wrong. I am
not there yet. Courage is not one of my strong points. That's
why I need to be repeatedly reminded of the reality of the

battle and that part of my identity in Christ is as one of His soldiers.

A Word to the Wounded

No message like this would be complete without speaking to the believer who is in genuine anguish and pain and says, "I'd like to love God with all my strength, but I don't have any strength left to give. I'd like to be more motivated, but I am wounded; I am bruised. I just need help."

First of all, I want to point out that the letter I quoted from earlier was written by a person whom you would not normally associate with tough, war-minded Christianity. This person was wounded for many years. Her story is an encouragement that severely wounded people are intended to, and eventually can, become soldiers too. Soldiers do become wounded, and it is right and good to expect the Church to function like a hospital. However, it is supposed to function like a military hospital that gets you ready to go back to the front lines. If you're looking for a civilian hospital that will get you ready to coast for the rest of your life, I hope for your sake that you never find it.

God also gave me another insight that I trust will be encouraging to you. So far we have focused on the word *all* in "Love God with all your strength." Have you considered the word *your* in that command as well? God doesn't say, "I want you to love God with all of Billy Graham's strength." He says, "I want you to love God with all *your* strength." It may not be as much as somebody else's, but provided it's all you've got, that's all He asks.

And so, even if it is from a hospital bed, cry out to Him with the psalmist, "Blessed are those whose strength is in you, / who have set their hearts on pilgrimage" (Psalm 84:5). What does it say afterwards? "They go from strength to strength, / till each appears before God in Zion" (84:7).

Josiah loved God with all of his heart, soul, mind and strength, because three things had gripped his heart: the warnings of judgment in light of the great privilege of worship; the possibility of missing a *kairos* moment for action that might never return again; and the reality of battle with an unrelenting and crafty opponent. I want to set him in contrast against two other rulers who come to my mind.

Josiah had a son named Jehoiakim. Many years later, he too was confronted with a scroll—this one written by Jeremiah the prophet. And as he sat in his winter home in front of a comfortable fire and Jeremiah's scroll was read to him, he took out his knife and cut the scroll to pieces, burning it in the fire. Then he went after Jeremiah's life. And he took a nation into exile with him. I also think of Felix, the governor before whom Paul waxed eloquent on righteousness, judgment and self-control. Talk about a *kairos* moment! But what does Felix say? "That's enough for now! You may leave. When I find it convenient, I will send for you" (Acts 24:25). The word *kairos* is in that verse too. Felix was looking for a "convenient" *kairos*. It never came.

You have before you the example of Josiah but also the awesome possibility of reacting like Jehoiakim and Felix. God wants you to drive home a stake of commitment to love God with all you've got. Will you do it? Do not miss your *kairos* moment.

Note

1. William Shakespeare, *Julius Caesar*, act IV, scene iii.

10.
Loving
the
Lost

Imagine that you are the vice president of sales for a company that manufactures and markets a product you really believe in. You are on your way to meet the regional sales manager for a city of a million people. About a year ago, you had met with this sales manager and mapped out a strategy for impacting that city with your product. Research had revealed the following:

- The northeastern part of the city had 250,000 people who were unaware of the product and had no contact with anyone who owned it.

- The northwestern side had 375,000 people with only a marginal awareness of your product (and therefore a distorted understanding of it) and so few actual owners of the product that there was little chance of contact with them.

- The southwestern section had 250,000 people with a moderate awareness of your product and a fair possibility of contact with owners of the product.

- The southeastern section had 125,000 people, many of whom actually owned this product. On your last visit, you and the sales manager had recruited 200 people who were so happy with this product that they wanted to be promoters and distributors.

When you meet with the sales manager a year later, this is what you find: He has taken 190 of those 200 people and—believe it or not—made them work in the southeast, with people who already own the product! Is this guy out of his mind?

He's taken eight of the remaining ten distributors and put them to work in the region of the city with people who already have a moderate awareness of the product and moderate contact with owners. He's assigned only two distributors to the section where people have a marginal and distorted understanding of your product and almost zero contact with owners. That leaves no one to work in that huge potential market sector of 250,000 people with no awareness of the product and no contact with those who own it. Aren't you tempted to fire the guy on the spot?

When you return to your office, you decide to see how the regional sales managers in other cities are doing. And to your horror, everywhere you find the same kind of foolish practice. One could hardly dignify it with the word *strategy*.

There must be something wrong, you realize, with the marketing research that drives this kind of sales technique. So you contact the research department and find that they have a full-time strategy team. You ask, "How much time do you spend developing strategy to reach this huge, untapped sector of the market?" Their answer: only one hour a week—one hour out of forty. It doesn't make sense to you, but that's the way it is.

Then you talk to the finance department, which allocates the research dollars. And you find that only $1 out of every $300 is devoted to reaching those with little or no knowledge of the product. Unbelievable! But it's the same all over the company: Only 3 out of every 100 hours of sales training are devoted to this sector; ninety-nine percent of the sales brochures are given out in areas where people already own the product.

If this were a TV show, the camera would probably fade out, showing you with your head buried in your hands, completely flabbergasted at how anybody could market a product this way.

What does this highly imaginary scenario, which would never happen in the real marketplace with a real product, have to do with loving our neighbor as ourselves—the second of Jesus' two commandments, which He said summarized all the Law and the prophets? As Larry King says when he fades out to a commercial, "Don't go away." Hang in there with me for a moment as I approach this matter from the proverbial left field.

A clever lawyer who first heard Jesus articulate this commandment immediately responded with, "Who's my neighbor?"

Jesus replied by telling the story of the Good Samaritan— how a traveler from Jerusalem to Jericho was beaten up by a gang of highway robbers and left to die, stripped of everything he had. A Levite—we might say a layman from a nearby church—walked by, neatly sidestepped the individual and kept going. So did a priest—or, shall we say, a pastoral staff member from the same church. Then came a Samaritan, a member of that half-breed group that Jesus' original audience didn't like; they avoided all social contact with them. He picked up the victim of the attack, looked after his physical needs and left him in someone else's care, paying that person to look after the victim.

The point of the story, of course, is simply this: According to Jesus, anybody in need is our neighbor. There are people in need right in your church. There are people in need in your community. And there are people in need all over the world.

In later chapters we'll look at what it means to love our neighbor in each of these categories, but right now, as we take a closer look at the second of Jesus' two great commandments, I want to focus on the farthest end of the spectrum. What does it mean to love those who are farthest away from us, people whom we will most likely never see?

I have two reasons to focus on this faraway group. First, because they bear among them the highest concentration of people who are like the man in Jesus' story—physically, emotionally and spiritually lost and dying. Second, because the Church today (including evangelicals, whose orthodox theology acknowledges this lostness more explicitly than other branches of Christianity) is full of Levites and priests who neatly dodge their way around these far-off neighbors whom we are called to love.

That sales strategy parable was simply a modern-day, proportionally accurate picture of how we "market" the gospel. Approximately one quarter of the world—over a billion people— have absolutely no contact with any Christians and have never heard the message of Jesus Christ. They are divided into over 3,000 people groups—*unreached* people groups.[1] A people group, according to Peter Wagner's useful definition, is the smallest group of individuals who are so culturally and linguistically united that the gospel can travel through them without having to cross additional cultural and linguistic barriers.

Another billion-plus people are in the second category— they have a vague, distorted understanding of Jesus Christ and for all practical purposes have no contact with a Christian. Then there are two other groups of people, one with a moderate understanding of the gospel and some possibility of contact with believers and another with the largest percentage of Christians and the lowest number of unevangelized people. The last group has maximum awareness of the gospel and maximum contact with Christians; in fact, they have had so much exposure that many are insulated against the gospel.

How are we doing in our job of loving our distant neighbors? About the same kind of job our imaginary sales manager was doing in that city. Did you know that ninety-five percent of all Christian activity is directed at Christians? Ninety-nine percent of all Christian literature is directed at Christians. Of the five percent that work to extend the gospel to the lost, eighty percent of them work in an area with moderate understanding of the gospel and moderate possibility of contact. Barely two percent of all Christian activity is carried out in regions with distorted, minimal understanding of the gospel and minimal contact with Christians. And of course, there is still this huge block of people with whom there is no contact and no possibility of it.

There are 300,000 churches in North America. Barely 9,000 of them, or 3 in 100, have any kind of a program or focus on this least-evangelized region. How about money? Less than a penny out of every dollar given by Christians goes to address the needs of unreached people groups. Ninety-nine cents goes to ministry to Christians.[2] There are 450 Christian congregations in the world for every unreached people group. It should be an easy, manageable task.

And yet, not only is there an incredible ignorance of the status of this group of people, but David Barrett has estimated that, on average, the annual per capita Christian giving to directly impact this quarter of the world is less than fifty cents per person. Why is it that a strategy we would never tolerate in the business world we happily tolerate (or remain ignorant of) when it comes to the Great Commission—unless we do not really believe that the eternal destiny of these men and women is at stake?

That is why I have decided to begin our study of loving our neighbor as ourselves by emphasizing the need for every believer to do his part to correct this unwarranted and incomprehensible imbalance when it comes to fulfilling our Lord's command to take the gospel into all the world. Of course, love for our neighbor is not really a matter of mushy, warm feelings. As John Dawson writes:

> Have you ever wondered what it feels like to have a love for the lost? This is a term that we use as part of our Christian jargon. Many believers search their hearts in condemnation, looking for the arrival of some feeling of

> benevolence that will propel them into bold evangelism.
> It will never happen. It is impossible to love "the lost."
> You can't feel deeply for an abstraction or a concept. You
> would find it impossible to love deeply an unfamiliar in-
> dividual portrayed in a photograph, let alone a nation or
> a race or something as vague as "all lost people."[3]

In light of this persuasive, if not undeniable, assertion of Dawson's, I have found C.S. Lewis' and Scott Peck's understanding of love much more to the point when it comes to loving the far-off lost billions. They say the same thing in different words. Love is a deliberate stretching of ourselves for the lasting good (be it spiritual, physical or emotional) of another person.

While statistics and analogies are helpful to establish some basic concepts and articulate needs, ultimately we have to lay a solid biblical foundation if we are going to accept the challenge to reach the unreached and persevere with hope in redressing the above imbalance of resources and apply Lewis' and Peck's understanding of love to the "far-off lost." Missiologists call this "frontier missions." What does the Bible say about frontier missions?

The Great Need

When the Lord Jesus Christ appeared to Saul on the road to Damascus, "re-christened" him with the name Paul and recommissioned him as an apostle, He gave him this charge:

> I have appeared to you to appoint you as a servant and as
> a witness of what you have seen of me and what I will
> show you. . . . I am sending you to them [the Gentiles] to
> open their eyes and turn them from darkness to light,
> and from the power of Satan to God, so that they may re-
> ceive forgiveness of sins. (Acts 26:16-18)

Jesus Himself says that their eyes are closed; they are in darkness; they are under the power of Satan and need to have their sins forgiven. That, by itself, ought to settle once and for all—for those who believe that Jesus Christ is God and Lord—any debate over whether these people are truly lost and hence need to hear the gospel.

How does Paul handle this commission? In Romans 15, at the end of nearly twenty years of ministry, he says, "So from Jerusalem all the way around to Illyricum"—in modern-day Turkey—"I have fully proclaimed the gospel of Christ. . . . But now . . . there is no more place for me to work in these regions" (15:19, 23).

That ought to startle us. How can Paul say that there's no more work for him to do when in that region there were still tens of thousands—maybe hundreds of thousands—who still had not become followers of Jesus Christ?

It is because Paul understood an important principle: There were churches in all those areas, spreading the good news. Even though the region was still unevangelized, it was no longer unreached. And Paul clearly understood the imperative behind Jesus' words: We can't keep on occupying ourselves forever with the unevangelized. Once they have been reached and a viable church has been planted, we need to move outward, to that quarter of the world where people have no contact and no churches at all. And so Paul says, "It has always been my ambition to preach the gospel where Christ was not known, so that I would not be building on someone else's foundation" (15:20).

For His Sake

The reality of human lostness and the need to keep pushing the gospel outward—those are the first two elements of the biblical mandate. But there is an even greater reason to focus on the unreached. In Romans 1:5 Paul says, "Through him and for his name's sake, we received grace and apostleship to call people from among all the Gentiles to the obedience that comes from faith."

The ultimate motive for learning to love our distant neighbors—or anybody else, for that matter—is "for His name's sake." More than their lostness, it is the glory of God's name that is at stake. He brings glory to Himself by powerfully saving men and women from every nation and every people group. John Dawson continues his previous observations on the difficulty of loving lost people with whom we have no relationship:

> Take those first steps in evangelism [or frontier missions, in our context] because you love God. It is not primarily out of a compassion for humanity that we share our faith or pray for the lost; it is first of all, love for God. . . . Humanity does not deserve the love of God any more than you or I do. We should never be Christian humanists, taking Jesus to poor sinful people, reducing Jesus to some kind of product that will better their lot. People deserve to be damned, but Jesus, the suffering Lamb of God, deserves the reward of his suffering.[4]

It's downright scary how humanistic we can become in our thinking without being aware of it.

Objection! This commission to frontier missions may apply to Paul and the other apostles, but does it apply to ordinary laypeople like us? Consider the wording of the Great Commission, which Jesus delivered at the end of his earthly ministry: "Therefore go and make disciples of all nations, baptizing them in the name of the Father and of the Son and of the Holy Spirit, and teaching them to obey everything I have commanded you. And surely I am with you always, to the very end of the age" (Matthew 28:19-20).

Obviously, this commission couldn't have been only for the disciples—they weren't going to live to the end of the age! But Jesus said, "I will be with you to the end of the age," underlining very clearly for us the fact that this commission—to take the gospel to the uttermost corners of the earth—is a continuing mandate for all those who would also come to believe in Jesus through the disciples, meaning you and me (pastors and laypeople).

What are the prospects for success in this mission? That's always good to know before we join an enterprise. Are we backing a winning or a losing cause? Jesus gives us a glimpse of what it will look like when everything's finished. In Revelation 5:9 we read,

> And they sang a new song:
> "You are worthy to take the scroll
>   and to open its seals,
> because you were slain,
>   and with your blood you purchased men for God
>   from every tribe and language and people and nation.
> You have made them to be a kingdom and priests
>   to serve our God."

This is the culmination of God's desire and unchanging commitment to glorify His name by calling out for Himself a people from every people group in the world who will worship the Lamb, Jesus Christ. The mission on which we have been sent is guaranteed to succeed.

Is it possible to love God with all our hearts, minds and strength but not love that cause that is closest to His own heart? Is it possible for a husband and a wife to love each other and have no interest at all in the things that are closest to each other's hearts? Is it possible for a parent to love a son or a daughter and not care at all about what makes his heart throb and what he sees as his reason for living? It's no different with God. We cannot love God and not love the mission that is closest to His heart.

Obstacles

Both the greatness of the need of our faraway neighbors and the unshakable commitment of God to call out a people for

Himself are great motives for us to learn to love the lost. But there are obstacles as well. The most crippling one is that of pessimism. We look at the sheer magnitude of the unreached—a billion-plus—and the massive engines of persecution and opposition that are arrayed against us in those very regions of the world with the highest concentration of the unreached, and we say, "What's the use? It's impossible!"

The only cure for pessimism is faith, and the only thing that builds faith is the Word of God. Faith comes by hearing the Word (see Romans 10:17). The ringing, recurring testimony of Scripture on this subject can destroy the crippling effect of pessimism in our lives. When Jesus' disciples said, "Who then can be saved?" He replied, "With man this is impossible, but not with God; all things are possible with God" (Mark 10:26-27).

God's power and ability to save any human being are unlimited. There is no one He sets His heart upon whom He cannot save. He said, "I have other sheep that are not of this sheep pen. I must bring them also. They too will listen to my voice, and there shall be one flock and one shepherd" (John 10:16). Look at the imperatives in these verses: "I have"; "I must"; "they will listen." The compassion of the Great Shepherd, the imperative within His heart and the declaration that those sheep not yet of this fold (Israel) will hear His voice are tremendous sustainers of optimism.

Yes, the task is difficult, seemingly insurmountable. But the power of God to save and the imperatives in Jesus' declaration are our ultimate source of optimism in this cause. This was illustrated in the life of a young man by the name of Peter Cameron Scott.[5] Born in Glasgow, Scotland, in 1867, he went to Africa as a missionary. In a short while he was so sick that he returned to England, a dejected man.

While waiting to recover his health, he said, "I will recommit myself to go to Africa." He did return eventually—and his joy was multiplied when his brother John went with him.

But his joy was turned to incredible sorrow when, within a few months, John got sick and died. Peter Cameron Scott buried his brother John in Africa, far away from his home.

Once again, he recommitted himself to preach the gospel in Africa. Once again, health problems plagued him and he returned to England—defeated, despairing and broken. Would he ever recover from this despondency? Would he ever get the strength to go back to Africa? One day he went to Westminster Abbey to pray and he sought out the tomb of David Livingstone, the great pioneer missionary. As he knelt to pray, he read this inscription on the tombstone: "I have other sheep that are not of this sheep pen. I must bring them also. They too will listen to my voice, and there shall be one flock and one shepherd" (John 10:16). And Peter Cameron Scott was revived, went back to Africa and founded the African Inland Mission, which would, for over a century, blaze a trail for the gospel in Africa.

Jesus Christ's unswerving commitment to call to Himself men and women from every nation restored a broken man and fulfilled his wish. John Piper, in his book *Let the Nations Be Glad*, says it will be no different for us:

> At the bottom of all our hope, when everything else has given way, we stand on this great reality: the everlasting, all sufficient God is infinitely, unwaveringly, and eternally committed to the glory of his great and holy name. For the sake of his fame among the nations he will act. His name will not be profaned for ever. The mission of the church will be victorious. He will vindicate his people and his cause in all the earth.[6]

This is the holy optimism that gets rid of the obstacle of pessimism.

But what do we do then? What form does loving those who are so far away from us take? The first and most concrete thing we can do to demonstrate our love for the unreached, in the

light of the impossibility of the task and the awesome commitment of God to His name, is to pray—to cry out to the Father
that He will "bare" His holy right arm of power before the nations, do the impossible and call out from among these very
people groups a people for Himself.

All through the decade of the 1990s (especially in the
months of October '93, '95, '97 and '99) millions of Christians all over the world gathered together in groups, small
and large, focusing their prayers on a particular region of the
world known as the 10/40 Window.[7] It is the area from 10
degrees north to 40 degrees north latitude from West Africa
to East Asia. When this effort started in October '93, ninety-
seven percent of the people in the fifty-five most unevangelized countries of the world lived inside this window. This
window also contained eighty-two percent of the poorest
people in the world. If you combine the two statistics, then
nearly ninety-nine percent of the lost poor in the world lived
inside the 10/40 Window.

One of the most effective things we can do for the cause of
the Great Commission is to join in prayer with our brothers
and sisters all over the world to tear down the strongholds inside the 10/40 Window. This immediately brings up a second
objection, however. If we really want to love these people, then
shouldn't we *do* something? After all, love is action, isn't it?
Why bother with prayer?

Brothers and sisters, we simply must get rid of the persistent notion in so many of our minds that praying is not
working. The uniform testimony of Scripture, of history and
of the giants of the faith has always been consistent: that
strategic, sustained, corporate, persistent, systematic, inter-
cessory prayer is hard work indeed. But it is how you strike
the blow on the battlefield. S.D. Gordon put it this way:
"Prayer strikes the blow and the servants pick up the pieces."

Is it just nice rhetoric or is it really true? Let me cite just
two of many examples that show the critical role of prayer.

Some years ago a group of North American Christians began to pray for an unreached people group that lived in a remote part of Asia. A few months later, they got a startling answer to their prayer. An American expedition was doing some mountain climbing in that remote part of Asia. They weren't missionaries—that wasn't even on their radar screen. They lost their way and stumbled upon this particular unreached people group. A Christian in that mountain-climbing party was able to initiate the introduction of the gospel to this unreached group.

A second example comes from the First Evangelical Free Church of Fullerton, in southern California. They "adopted" an unreached people group known as the Dai, who live in the Yunan province of China. They began to pray that God would mobilize Chinese Christians to catch a burden for the Dai people. Little did they know that at the same time there was a group of Christians in China who were praying for God to show them where to concentrate their evangelistic efforts. Some time after that, a group of these praying Christians from the Fullerton church took a trip to China and met some of the Chinese Christians who'd been praying for wisdom. And when these Christians heard that this church was praying for the Dai people, they got their answer! Now there is a work among the Dai people. Prayer still strikes the decisive blow and gets the action, the proper action in harmony with God's agenda, rolling.

Now it almost goes without saying (and that's why I am saying it) that loving our farthest neighbors by becoming active participants in frontier missions involves far more than prayer. It involves building relationships with those who are serving cross-culturally so that our prayers can be more heartfelt, strategic and intelligent and so that we can encourage them to persevere in a hard task. It involves giving of our material resources so that these workers can be transported and supported and their children educated, their health needs taken care of, etc. It might involve visiting them in their countries of work so that we can get a firsthand look at what they are doing and who they are reaching with the gospel.

To keep this chapter to a reasonable length, I have chosen to focus on prayer, because it is foundational to fueling the rest. I would encourage you to read my book *World Christians: Living on the Wavelength of the Great Commission* for a book-length amplification of this chapter, not because it is the best book on the subject, but because it is the simplest.[8] It was written specifically to give Christians not yet "hooked up" to frontier missions some practical first steps that they can take in one or more of these various ways of getting involved.

Is there a cost to all this? Of course. For starters, there is the cost of reordered priorities, of investing time that we spend doing other things. There is the cost of moving out of our comfort zones as we gather in small groups to pray. There is the cost of learning the kinds of things that this chapter has been setting forth so that we can understand the plight of those who live inside the 10/40 Window. There is the cost of beginning to suffer a little, of allowing God to squeeze our hearts just a little so that they ache for and with our brothers and sisters inside the Window who are working under threatened or actual persecution, facing desperate odds, to communicate the gospel to those who haven't heard. In S.D. Gordon's words, they are not able to "pick up the pieces" because very few of us are "striking the decisive blow."

It will cost, but don't think of it as sacrifice. Jesus is not asking you to *ultimately* sacrifice anything. Consider Mark 10:28-30, where Peter said to Jesus, "We have left everything to follow you!" Jesus didn't say, "Well done—such a wonderful sacrifice!" No, Jesus corrected his perspective:

> I tell you the truth . . . no one who has left home or brothers or sisters or mother or father or children or fields for me and the gospel will fail to receive a hundred times as much in this present age (homes, brothers, sis-

ters, mothers, children and fields—and with them, perse-
cutions) and in the age to come, eternal life.

Jesus is saying, "Peter, don't tell me you've sacrificed anything, because I am no person's debtor. There is nothing you
give me that I will not give back to you—pressed down,
shaken together, in full measure, overflowing. When it is all
done, difficulties and all, you will never be able to say that
you are My benefactor. I am the benefactor; you are eternally
the beneficiary." A man who understood this dimension of
"no ultimate sacrifice" was David Livingstone:

> People talk of the sacrifice I have made in spending so
> much of my life in Africa. Is that a sacrifice which brings
> its own best reward in helpful activity, the consciousness
> of doing good, peace of mind and a bright hope of a glori-
> ous destiny hereafter? Say rather that it is a privilege.
> Anxiety, sickness, suffering or danger now and then with
> a foregoing of the common charities of this life may
> make us pause and cause the spirit to waver and the soul
> to sink, but let this only be for a moment. All these are
> nothing when compared with the glory which shall be re-
> vealed in and for us. I never made a sacrifice.[9]

It is all the more remarkable when we stop to reflect that this
statement came from a man who buried a wife and two children in Africa. You and I will never be David Livingstones, but
I think we can at least begin to catch the spirit of what he was
saying and what is reflected in Jesus' words.

So pray for the lost of this world—but not because you feel
guilty. Don't pray because of what somebody else will think
of your Christianity if you refuse. Above all, don't pray because you think you are making a great sacrifice. Pray because the revelation of God's glory in redeeming lost men
and women and the joy that will be yours as He is worshiped
by the redeemed will satisfy the deepest longings of your
heart as nothing else can.

I will never forget the testimony of a Christian woman who, even when facing major challenges in her marriage and the waywardness of one of her adult children, said to my wife, "The only time I really feel peace is when I pray for _____" (a young couple who were proclaiming Christ to a very resistant people group inside the 10/40 Window).

Whatever you invest in frontier missions, in learning to love our farthest-away neighbors, remember this: Jesus will not remain your debtor. Pray with the declaration of Piper ringing in your heart:

> God is pursuing with omnipotent passion a worldwide purpose of gathering joyful worshipers for himself from every tribe and tongue and people and nation. He has an inexhaustible enthusiasm for the supremacy of his name among the nations. Therefore, let us bring our affections into line with his, and, for the sake of his name, let us renounce the quest for worldly comforts, and join his global purpose. If we do this, God's omnipotent commitment to his name will be over us like a banner, and we will not lose, in spite of many tribulations (Acts 9:16; Romans 8:35-39).[10]

Notes

1. These numbers are the correct order of magnitude, even though the precise figures may be out of date. To God's glory, much progress has been made since the preaching of this material several years ago.
2. Again, these figures are from several years ago. While precise numbers may have changed, the imbalance implied exists today.
3. John Piper, *Let the Nations Be Glad* (Grand Rapids: Baker, 1993), pp. 38-9, quoting John Dawson, *Taking Our Cities for God* (Lake Mary, FL: Charisma House, 1989), pp. 208-9.
4. Ibid.
5. Ibid.
6. Piper, pp. 36-7.
7. For more information on the 10/40 Window, see George Otis, Jr. and Mark Brockman, eds., *Strongholds of the 10/40 Window* (Seattle: YWAM Publishing, 1995).
8. Sunder Krishnan, *World Christians: Living on the Wavelength of the Great Commission* (Toronto: Clements Publishing, 2001).
9. From a speech given at Cambridge University on December 4, 1857.
10. Piper, p. 40.

11.
Your Nearby Neighbor

Imagine, if you will, the most brilliant person you know coming to Jesus with a profound question, one that he hopes will stimulate a lively, enjoyable, intellectual discussion. This is just what happened in Luke 10:25-37. An expert in the law asked, "What must I do to inherit eternal life?" Jesus responded with a question, the answer to which the expert probably learned in the third grade: "What does the Law say?"

What an insult! An intellectual in a position like that gets embarrassed and defensive; I can just see this expert spitting out the answer: "Love God with all your heart, soul, mind and strength, and love your neighbor as yourself." And to make matters worse, even then there isn't any discussion. Jesus simply cuts things short by saying, "Well, then, just go and do it. Love God, love your neighbor. End of discussion."

Now the expert in the law has an objection! He must have been thinking, *Just a minute! You're going too fast here, Jesus. We haven't defined our terms yet. And you know what happens if we don't define things properly. What if I rush out and love somebody, only to find that he isn't my neighbor?* So he asked, "And who is my neighbor?"

In answer to that question, Jesus tells the story of the Good Samaritan, concluding with the words, "Go and do likewise." It is as if he were saying, "Stop theorizing, please; stop your discussions; just go and obey. Whoever is in need is your neighbor, and to meet his need as best you can is to love him."

In the last chapter we began to look at what loving our neighbor as ourselves means for those neighbors who are farthest away from us—those who are desperately lost and poor, who have no opportunity to hear the gospel and have no contact with Christians. We necessarily had to struggle with concepts like unreached people groups and distribution of resources. And we learned that, first and foremost, one thing (but not the only thing) we can do to love people like that is to pray—to cry out to the sovereign God, who is committed to honoring and glorifying His name among every people group in the world.

But in this chapter I want to focus closer to home. We have to think globally but act locally. What does it mean to love our *nearby* neighbor, those right next to us? Rebuked by Jesus' words to the expert in the law, let's not do much conceptualizing and theorizing here; instead let us reflect the emphasis of Jesus and focus much more on "going and doing likewise." It's a simple commandment; it's not hard to understand. Your neighbor is anybody in need, and to love him is to minister to that need. How did we ever succeed in complicating it so much? As a starting point, meditate on this paragraph from C.S. Lewis' essay "The Weight of Glory":

> It is a serious thing to live in a society of possible gods and goddesses, to remember that the dullest and most uninteresting person you talk to may one day be a creature which, if you saw it now, you would be strongly tempted to worship, or else a horror and a corruption such as you now meet, if at all, only in a nightmare. . . . There are no ordinary people. You have never talked to a mere mortal. . . . But it is immortals whom we joke with, work with, marry, snub and exploit—immortal horrors or everlasting splendors. . . . Next to the Blessed Sacrament itself, your neighbor is the holiest object presented to your senses.[1]

Jesus saw people like that. And if we are to love our neighbor as ourselves, the first thing we have to do is to see people the way Jesus sees them. The disciples had to repeatedly learn this lesson. When mothers brought their little children to Jesus so that He could bless them, the disciples shooed them away (see Mark 10:13). Right after that incident, Mark recounts the story of the rich young ruler who wanted to see Jesus. I wonder if the disciples saw him hanging around waiting to speak to Jesus, so they shooed away the mothers and their children to let the important man get to the front of the line!

Jesus wouldn't have any of that; He blessed the little children. Of course, that doesn't mean that He didn't care about the rich man as well. In fact, Mark 10:21 says, "Jesus looked at him and loved him. 'One thing you lack,' he said. 'Go, sell everything you have and give to the poor, and you will have treasure in heaven. Then come, follow me.' "

Jesus displayed the same concern in the healing of Bartimaeus (see 10:46-52). He and the disciples were on their way to Jerusalem, where events of truly cosmic significance were poised to happen and a global movement was about to be initiated, when a blind man cried out, "Jesus, Son of David, have mercy on me!" This time the crowd, not the disciples, took on the role of the indignant protectors of Jesus' precious time and told the blind man to be quiet. But again Jesus stopped and healed him.

When he healed the leper in Mark 1:40-42, it was not merely with a word, which we know would have been sufficient; He also touched him. Dr. Paul Brandt, who has worked with lepers in India, says that in touching the leper, Jesus showed that He was sensitive not only to the man's physical need but also to his emotional need—the deep-seated sense of isolation that comes from a lifetime of not being touched.

Can you imagine what it would be like to have leprosy and never to be touched by anyone but those who are similarly diseased? Jesus showed His compassion to this man not just by healing him but by reaching out and touching him.

Every single individual bore "the weight of glory" for Jesus. This was effectively captured in a powerful one-liner whose source I have long forgotten: "For Jesus, even crowds were simply multiplied opportunities for individual conquest."

A Second Touch

In the case of the man who was born blind (see Mark 8:22-26), Jesus healed him by touching him twice. The first time the man saw people like trees walking around, and the second time he saw them clearly. Most of us are like that. To see people as Jesus sees them, we need a second touch. We've had one touch from God and we see people like trees. Trees are good for shade, for wood, for fruit; they are useful to us. But it's not until we are touched a second time that "tree" people (who may be useful to us) become people for whom we can be of some use.

Of course, that begs a question; Jesus isn't here in the flesh anymore. We can't run to Him literally and say, "Put spit upon my eyes and help me see." How do we get the second touch?

It's confession time for me at this point. Most of the things I say from the pulpit (some of which get written down in a book) I have worked hard to think through, apply and internalize in my life. But when it comes to seeing people as people, when it comes to loving my neighbor, there are many in my congregation who are far ahead of me on the journey. As I watch them, I am struck by the relative coldness and hardness of my own heart and my inability to love as they love. And it stirs within me a fresh longing for a second touch.

All I can do is to set before you what I have learned as I have observed people who love so beautifully. The stories I've read and the people I know personally have given me some clues of how God might touch us a second time. I want to set before you five different ways in which God may touch us, in the hope that they will stimulate your own hunger and give shape to your prayers for the second touch.

A Chance Encounter

One way that a second touch may come is through *a chance encounter*. Bob McCallister was the deputy director and chief of staff for the governor of South Carolina for many years. Halfway through his second marriage, wilting under the pressures of a job that threatened to tear him apart emotionally, he gave his life to Jesus Christ. One day as he was driving along a busy street, he saw traffic up ahead being diverted by some obstacle. As he got closer he saw that it was a man in a wheelchair, pushing himself along with all his might. McCallister did something that he had never done before: He stopped and asked if he could help. With sweat pouring from his forehead, arms limp, feet hanging like useless matchsticks, the man in the wheelchair said, "My name is Odell. There are two women who live in a shanty nearby that are both sick. I'm going to the rescue mission to get food for them." It was a seven-and-a-half-mile round-trip!

McCallister packed Odell and his wheelchair into his car, drove to the rescue mission, picked up the food, went back and visited these two women. But for weeks afterward, he couldn't get Odell and the two women out of his mind, and he kept asking himself this question: "When have you ever given everything you've got for some other human being?" Bob McCallsiter was beginning to feel for the first time the pain of God's heart for the unloved and the unlovable. He signed up as a volunteer at a nearby Christian shelter for abused women. That led to an invitation to visit an African-American, Muslim prisoner on death row in a nearby prison, which McCallister accepted.

Slowly word began to spread, and one by one other prisoners began to ask McCallister to visit them. Bob had suddenly found his calling: sharing the gospel with men on death row. His new vision for service and renewed faith spilled over to his wife, Carol, who now assists him in his ministry. "Without Odell," Bob said, "I wonder if anything further would really have happened in our Christian lives."[2]

A chance encounter can lead to a second touch as God plunks the Odells of this world in our way and begins to paralyze us by the burden that this creates.

Childhood Preparation

A very different kind of story concerns a young woman named Sherry Woods. As a little girl growing up in Minnesota, her hero was Martin Luther King, Jr. She would scan the newspapers every day for stories about this preacher from Atlanta. She would cut out all the stories and paste them in her scrapbook. When she heard the line in his famous "I Have a Dream" speech about black children and white children playing together, something within her said, "Yes, that's the way it's got to be."

Sherry Woods is now an adult, a white member in a predominantly black, lower-middle-class church, directing a program known as Unique. On Tuesday evenings, when the lights of Third City Church come on, hoards of youngsters from that community converge upon that church, and every one of them is assigned a volunteer as their tutor. For the next three hours these kids, for perhaps the only time that week, have the undivided attention of an adult. The tutors come both from Sherry's church and from a white congregation up the street that is made up of diplomats and lawyers.

Kids from the program are now in college, including a girl by the name of Tenisha. One night, two teenagers drove by and sprayed the sidewalk with bullets, hitting Tenisha. As she lay there close to death, the tutors and students of Unique prayed. Tenisha recovered, and today she is working on her master's degree in college. And so is her brother.

What's happened to these two congregations in the meantime? Upper-class whites and lower-class blacks are learning to love each other as denominational walls are crumbling in the process. The second touch often comes by *a unique preparation in childhood* when God gets ahold of the hearts of young men and women in their early years.[3]

Inspired Leadership

The second touch comes a third way too—from *inspired leadership*. John Aker was a pastor in Rockville, Illinois. One phrase his close associates used to describe him became part of my prayer language—they said that he was a man who "bubbles with the Holy Spirit." I regularly asked God for quite a while after I read this story to make me bubble with the Holy Spirit too.

On Friday mornings, John went out with several volunteers from his church to what had been a nearby elementary school—only now it was an abortion clinic. He and several children would march for a couple of hours—quietly and well behaved. They sang, prayed and lit candles.

Fred was a guard at the abortion clinic. It would have been easy to hate Fred. His face disfigured by an explosion in a high school chemistry lab, he was an alcoholic who got red in the face and swore a blue streak. So John Aker crossed the picket line one day and said to him, "Fred, I know I'm from the opposition, but I want to be your friend. I'm not gonna turn my back on you when I meet you in the supermarket. But, Fred, I have a mother and two young daughters on that picket line; will you please watch your language?"

Fred grunted.

As winter approached, it got a lot colder, so they would bring hot cocoa and doughnuts to the picket lines. By now the children were slowly beginning to lose their fear of Fred; children are usually the first ones to do that. They discovered that Fred didn't have a family, and since it was Christmas-time they started saving their pocket money and badgering their parents for extra change. On the Friday before Christmas, they came to Fred and asked for his permission to cross the picket line. With a cup of hot cocoa in one hand, doughnuts in the other and a beautifully gift-wrapped package, they said, "Fred, here's your Christmas present." Fred spoke for the first time and said, "Thank you."

A few weeks later, Pastor John was at a board meeting in his church when a knock came at the door. It was Fred—drunk, but wanting to talk to the pastor. The board meeting was immediately canceled; the pastor and assistant pastor sat up all night in a restaurant with Fred while the alcohol wore off. There in that restaurant he bowed his head and gave his heart to Jesus Christ. Someone in the congregation arranged for a job for Fred, while others paid off his outstanding debts. And Fred's life began to change.

The story doesn't have a happy ending, because the owner of the abortion clinic tempted Fred with alcohol and lured him back to his old job. But the relationship did not end; John continued to talk to Fred and even have lunch or dinner with him.

I will not easily forget what Pastor John said about his friendship with Fred: "The success is that the relationship is intact. People need to see Jesus, God in us, enfleshed again. So with Fred, I've built a friendship, a bridge of kindness he can walk over. I'll meet him on it any time."[4] The second touch can come through inspired pastoral leadership. But don't wait for the Holy Spirit to set your pastor bubbling! It can also come through lay leadership. He might set you bubbling first and teach others through you.

Gifts and Accountability

There are two more ways that the second touch can come. I want you to see them in action, illustrated by someone in the congregation I am privileged to serve.

Paula had a passion for photography, so when her brother, who worked at an inner-city mission, asked her to take some pictures for a new brochure to help send kids to camp from the inner city, she readily agreed to join him at the camp for the day to photograph the facilities and the children. "It was the joy on the faces of these children that inspired me to come back for longer than one day," Paula said. She and her brother made plans to go to the camp the next summer and to bring some teenagers from the inner city with them. Paula volunteered to be the camp cook.

One month prior to leaving, however, she developed severe pain in her neck and back, a relapse of an old problem. She had to phone her brother and tell him to find someone to replace her. "It was a very discouraging time for me," she said. "I didn't quite understand why this was happening."

God had other plans for her, however. One week before camp her brother called with excitement in his voice. The cooking position had been filled, but photography had just been added to the camp program; despite her chronic pain, would she consider teaching the kids? Read on as Paula tells the rest of the story:

> At this point, I knew God was leading me. On the Sunday prior to leaving, as a step of obedience, I asked to be anointed with oil at church so that God could use me at this camp. I also asked for prayer support from my small group on Wednesday evening. I woke up on Thursday morning for the first time in months without pain, able to prepare for leaving. This was my first time working at a Bible camp and little did I know what an impact this week would have on my life. Along with kids from the mission were teenagers from all walks of life, Christian and non-Christian, totaling about 150 students, ages fifteen to seventeen. So much happened that week, but the highlight was watching the transformation of these kids.
>
> I thought I was going to camp because of my passion for photography, but God used my spiritual gift of mercy. I

began building relationships with a few of the girls and it didn't take long to see God's plan for me unfold before my eyes. I have a real burden for those who are hurting; many of these girls shared stories of abuse, both physical and emotional. Some have had abortions; many come from divorced families and alcoholic homes. The overall yearning in these girls' lives was to have a loving relationship with their fathers.

God was closing doors and opening new ones for me. If I had worked at the camp as a cook, the job would not have enabled me to form relationships with the girls because of the time involved in cooking. As a result of the Holy Spirit moving in the chapel services in the evenings, I spent many a night holding these girls in my arms while they cried and cried. Often they could not express the hurt in their lives, so I would just hold them and cry with them, and pray that they would come to know Jesus Christ as their loving Father.

One girl that comes to mind in particular is Crystal, a Native Indian girl. The entire time at camp she never smiled at all. You could see the hurt written all over her face. It wasn't until we had an open forum on suffering, where many of the counselors gave testimony to God's grace and mercy in their lives, that the change came. One particular testimony relating to abortion broke through to Crystal and she began to cry.

That evening her counselor and I held her while she wept in our arms, unable to share what was on her heart. This was the second to last night at camp. On the last night, during worship time, Crystal was sitting in front of me. She turned around and looked up at me—beaming with a smile on her face that I had never seen before! She looked so different—beautiful, radiant. I will never forget that moment as I knew she had just opened her heart to Christ. We held each other with tears of joy for the first time.

On the boat home the next morning, I watched her laughing with the other girls who had also become Christians. The boat that traveled home was filled with so much love and joy. I was witnessing God's grace and love before my eyes.

I am so thankful to God for leading me to the camp and for the opportunities He gave me to use my spiritual gifts. This has confirmed a vision I have had for a long time to have a home for street kids which would incorporate my spiritual gifts of mercy and hospitality. I have received so many blessings from using my spiritual gifts. I have learned to really trust in God and He has given me confidence to move forward with this vision.

Sunder has taught us that we can lose a vision if it is not kept alive. And I praise God that it grows stronger each day. In order to keep this vision alive, I have turned down two job opportunities that were unrelated to it. I am also taking classes in youth ministry at a local Bible college and volunteering at a drop-in center for teenagers.

I also believe that to keep a vision alive we need accountability and prayer. I am thankful to everyone in my small group and in my church for letting me share this vision and for encouraging me to move ahead with it. I praise God for His healing and enabling to pursue His plan for me. I hope this has been an encouragement to you to step out in faith and use the spiritual gifts that God has so lovingly given you. Using my spiritual gifts has set me free to dream. I encourage you to allow God to be the ultimate dream fulfiller in your lives.[5]

Paula's life illustrates beautifully the fourth and the fifth methods by which God brings the second touch: *using one's gifts and talents to meet specific needs* and *accountability to a caring community*. Paula had a passion for the poor, a gift of mercy and a talent for photography. She made herself accountable to others—a small as well as a larger group of people. She had made a commitment to let God use her, and they did not let her forget it. They prayed with her and for her, and God kept opening doors. The community helped her to find her gifts and kept her accountable to use them.

Some of you are like Paula and don't need chapters like this to inspire you to love your neighbors. You could tell your own stories to illustrate many more ways in which the second touch can come to people. For the rest of us, if we are to obey Jesus' command to love our neighbor as ourselves, we have to begin at the beginning—we need the second touch. We have to keep praying that the Lord Jesus Christ will touch our eyes so that we stop seeing people as trees walking around and begin to see them as bearers of the eternal weight of glory. And as we pray, if we stay alert to the chance encounter; if we let our childhood dreams begin to surface once again; if we take the first halting, even fearful, steps along the paths set out for us by inspired leadership; if we respond to requests in keeping with our gifts and talents; if we make ourselves accountable to a community, we can dare to believe that the second touch will come. And when it comes, we are more likely to take advantage of it.

Every election season, the newspapers and airwaves are full of politicians making promises that we know they are not going to keep. In that context, I would like to conclude with an observation by Charles Colson in his book *Who Speaks for God*. He had just been to an inner-city service in Atlanta, Georgia, where the community was bidding good-bye to six convicts who had spent two weeks refurbishing the homes of two elderly widows. They had grown to love each other in the process. And so, after that wonderful service, Colson got on a plane and headed back home. He picked up the newspaper and read about the budget deadlock in Washington. A Democratic Congress and a Republican president had locked horns for nine months; now, two months into the new fiscal year, there was still no budget. Listen to Colson's observations on that situation:

> In Washington, the most powerful nation on earth seemed almost paralyzed. In Atlanta, some folks saw a need, quickly got busy and met it. . . . The contrast is in-

structive. It yields an important insight into our troubled times.

Government in a democracy is but a mirror reflection of the people. Consequently the budget impasse is but a symptom of a deeper malaise. One wonders whether egocentrism and materialism are so infiltrating the American value structure as to sap our nation of its capacity to act, to rise above partisan or selfish interests. The willingness to pull together for the common good is, after all, the cement which holds the loose bricks of democracy together.

That willingness, in the final analysis, is a question of human spirit and purpose; indeed a moral question. So, too, the answer to the dilemma of these times is a moral answer. Our renewed sense of responsibility—of caring about one another—will come not from power-seeking politicians, but from the heart of compassionate individuals. And Christians must set clear examples of that caring.[6]

May God take our hearts in His hand and squeeze until we begin to feel a small part of His compassion for the unloved and the destitute. May the stories in this chapter (and may you come across many others like them) give shape and substance to our prayers so that we all will increasingly "bubble with the Holy Spirit" and the desperately needy community around us can receive love for the first time.

Notes

1. C.S. Lewis, "The Weight of Glory," in *The Weight of Glory* (New York: Macmillan, 1949), pp. 14-5.
2. Charles Colson, *The Body* (Dallas: Word, 1992), pp. 385-7.
3. Ibid., pp. 350-1.
4. Ibid., pp. 354-7.
5. This is an edited transcript of Paula's testimony, given at a Sunday morning service at Rexdale Alliance Church, Toronto, Ontario.
6. Charles Colson, *Who Speaks for God?* (Wheaton, IL: Good News Publishers, 1985), pp. 161-2.

12.

Loving
the
Bride

One of my many pleasurable pastoral responsibilities is officiating at weddings. Most weddings have two stages: the rehearsal and then the real thing, usually the day after. If you were to drop in during a rehearsal and you didn't know the bridal party, it is not likely that you would be able to pick out the bride. She's far from the resplendent beauty that she will be the next day. She is very ordinary—dressed in street clothes, her hair not done up the way it will be the next day. She is probably somewhat frazzled and nervous; maybe one of the bridesmaids is late, or the groom, as usual, has forgotten something that he was supposed to do. And all of these things are written large upon the bride's face.

But the next day is completely different. Everyone knows who the bride is; all eyes are upon her. I love to watch the bridegroom when he catches sight of her for the first time, decked out in her bridal glory. And as she comes close enough for their eyes to meet, the intensity of the emotion they feel is palpable, and I often find myself swallowing an unexpected lump in my throat.

This oft-repeated scene is a powerful metaphor for another wedding—the one between Jesus Christ and His Bride, the Church. The difference with that wedding is that we've only seen the Bride at the rehearsal and can't even begin to comprehend the resplendence of her glory on the wedding day. Imagine my shock, therefore, when I came across this statis-

tic: *The Journal of the Evangelical Theological Society*, in thirty-
four years of publication, has devoted only one issue to the
doctrine of the Church.

This deplorable imbalance in our theology has led to a
dangerous omission. While it is important and appropriate
for us to see ourselves individually as bearers of the image of
God, we have tragically forgotten, if we ever remembered,
the corresponding equal need to see ourselves collectively as
His Bride, the Church.

Imagine that you've come to a wedding. The Groom—Jesus
Christ—is right here, dressed in all His military splendor,
girded with majesty, with His sword upon His side (see Psalm
45 for the origin of this image). The wedding processional is
about to begin; soon the Bride will enter. And you're straining
your neck, as we all do at weddings, to catch at least a glimpse
of the Bride in all her glory. All of a sudden, you realize you're
looking at yourself; you're really not a guest at the wedding—
you're the Bride! What does Jesus see when He sees us, the
Church, coming down the aisle? We need a second touch from
God to see this, just as we need it to see people as bearers of the
weight of glory, headed for an eternity with God or apart from
God. Only this time I don't have to guess where the second
touch is coming from. The Holy Spirit directed the Apostle
Paul to write a letter to the Ephesians for the express purpose
of touching our eyes so that we can see the Bride of Christ the
way that Jesus Christ sees us.

In the very first chapter, the Apostle Paul says, "I pray also
that the eyes of your heart may be enlightened in order that
you may know the hope to which he has called you" (1:18).
The hope of the Christian is multifaceted, but Paul almost
certainly has one thing in mind, since in verse 5 he has said,
"He predestined us to be adopted as his sons through Jesus
Christ."

The word *adoption* in the English language has only one
common meaning, but it was not so in the first century. In

that era there was another, perhaps even more dominant, usage of the word *adoption*. It referred to the time when Roman sons were publicly acknowledged to have come of adult age. Lloyd C. Douglas, in his book *The Robe*, describes that ceremony through the eyes of the character Marcellus. As his father makes a speech to welcome him into Roman citizenship and to explain the responsibilities it entails, Marcellus feels as if his life has just begun.[1]

That's one idea that Paul conveys when he says that we are predestined for adoption. The day is coming when all believers in the Lord Jesus Christ collectively will be invested, in a public ceremony, with sonship—adulthood. In that day we will say, as Marcellus said, "I never lived till now. Life has begun."

Paul moves on to give us a second image. He not only prays that we will see the hope of our calling but "the riches of his glorious inheritance in the saints" (1:18). Notice that he is not talking about *our* inheritance but *Christ's* inheritance (if the NIV translation is correct). Jesus Christ is going to receive His glorious inheritance on *that* day. Do you know who the inheritance will be? *You and me*—the Church! Jesus Christ will delight in us as His rich inheritance, like no one ever did before. And Paul's prayer is that we might *now* know the richness that Christ sees in us, the Church—His inheritance.

He also prays that we may know "his incomparably great power *for us* who believe. That power is like the working of his mighty strength, which he exerted in Christ when he raised him from the dead and seated him at his right hand in the heavenly realms" (1:19-20). How is Christ's resurrection power *for* us? Paul tells us in 2:6-7, "And God raised us up with Christ and seated us with him in the heavenly realms in Christ Jesus, in order that in the coming ages he might show the incomparable riches of his grace."

When the Lord Jesus Christ was raised from the dead by the power of God and ascended into the presence of the Father, it only looked like He was separated from the watching disciples. In fact, something wonderful happened when Jesus rose from the dead and ascended. He gathered all of His people up with Him so that we are now seated together with Him. And it implies very clearly, of course, that we are seated on the throne with the Lord Jesus Christ, far above all principalities and powers.

To switch back to our wedding metaphor, if you will, it is the time when the Bride and Groom arrive at the reception and go to the head table—the Groom in His radiant glory and the Bride, the Church of Jesus Christ, sitting next to Him. And who are the guests? The principalities and the powers—all the hosts of heaven and hell. The spirit kingdom, good and bad, will be watching this, and their jaws will drop in proverbial amazement as they gasp at the sheer beauty of the Bride, whom Paul further describes in this way: "For we are God's workmanship" (2:10).

Greek scholars tell us that the word translated "workmanship" is close to the English word *poem*. A poet uses his or her mastery of language to juxtapose words in a way not normally encountered in mere prose; the resulting creation plays on the slumbering chords of emotions within us so that we feel what we formerly only understood with our minds. Could Paul be saying that each individual Christian is like a phrase, a line, a stanza, a metaphor that God has knit together, along with other Christians, into a magnificent poem that could affect its "readers" like a Shakespeare or a Tennyson masterpiece? Aren't you excited to know that this is how Jesus Christ thinks of you, the Church?

How will the Bride become so beautiful as to ravish the Bridegroom on their wedding day? She doesn't look so good these days, sometimes. Paul tells us how: "Christ loved the church and gave himself up for her to make her holy . . . and to present her to himself as a radiant church, without stain or wrinkle or any other blemish" (5:25-27). The Bride will be beautiful because Jesus Christ will have made her beautiful, through His death and through His life.

Paul seems to be ransacking the Greek language to somehow enable us to see how Jesus sees the Church. And he comes up with a brand-new metaphor in Ephesians 2:20-21. We, the Church, are "built on the foundation of the apostles and prophets, with Christ Jesus himself as the chief cornerstone. In him the whole building is joined together and rises to become a holy temple in the Lord." That one phrase, "joined together," is unique; again, if my scholarly sources are right (and where would I, a mere pastor, be if they aren't?), this phrase occurs only here in the New Testament and not at all in contemporary Greek writings of the time. Paul apparently had to fabricate a word to be able to paint this new picture of the Church. He takes three words that mean "join," "together" and "choose carefully" and fuses them into one.

Let me illustrate the meaning of this word in this way: If you are building a brick wall, you don't need to choose the bricks carefully. One brick is exactly like another; any brick will do as the next brick to go on the wall. But if you're building a stone fireplace, you put down the first one and slap the mortar on it, and then when you pick up the second one, it may not fit at all because each stone has radically different contours. So you throw it away and look through the heap and say, "Ah, this one." It's different from the first, but the contours match perfectly, so the two will fit together. Then you go to the pile once again, pick up another one and say, "That isn't good either; now I want one that is neither like the first one nor like the second one. It can't just fit the first one or just fit the second one; it has to fit the first and the second in combination." And so the third one goes into place. That way you carefully build the fireplace of deliberately chosen stones that are joined together.

That is the process Paul applies to the "building" that is the Church. When the Church is complete, she will not look like a brick wall, every brick monotonously the same. She will be like a magnificent cathedral built of granite hunks. No one stone will be like the other, yet each will have been chosen to fit the others perfectly, until the whole is an edifice that makes those who see it gasp in awe. Think of the biggest, most magnificent cathedral you've ever seen. The astonishment and awe you felt will be nothing compared to what the principalities and powers are going to feel when they see the Church on that final day.

Paul hasn't finished yet. In chapter 3 he says, "His [God's] intent was that now, through the church, the manifold wisdom of God should be made known to the rulers and authorities in the heavenly realms" (3:10). Focus on the word *manifold* for a minute. Our friendly scholars tell us that the word was used in those days to describe the different colors of a rich tapestry or outer garment, as in Joseph's "coat of many colours" (Genesis 37:3, KJV). Paul applies that to the Church. Every aspect of the Church's diversity—her ethnicity, languages, giftedness, etc.—will demonstrate yet another aspect of God's wisdom to the spiritual powers in the heavenly realms.

Put it all together and what do you get? How does Jesus see His Bride just as she's about to walk down the aisle? He sees us as a group coming of age and therefore being invested publicly with adulthood. He sees us as a holy and radiant Bride. He sees us as a carefully crafted poem that has been put together in such a way that it calls for the admiration of the gathered onlookers. He sees us as a carefully crafted building before which the most magnificent cathedral pales into insignificance. And He sees us as a multicolored, skillfully woven garment whose variety reflects the incredible wisdom of God.

Once you begin to see the Church that way, can you ever again be casual or critical about it? (I mean destructively critical.) The next time you are in a worship service, look out among the congregation and silently rehearse these words in your mind:

> You and I are one day going to take part in a public investiture ceremony like that of Marcellus that will make all the pomp and pageantry of Rome seem beggarly by com-

parison. You and I are one day going to be handed over together to Christ as a beautiful, treasured inheritance. You and I are going to be seated one day as Christ's Bride, holy and radiant. You and I are going to be like a carefully crafted poem, a brilliantly woven tapestry or a magnificently built cathedral, all of which will make the principalities and powers in heaven and in hell gasp in sheer wonder and amazement.

After you have done that, think about my question again. Can you ever again be casual about your relationships with your brothers and sisters in Christ? When we talk about loving our neighbor as ourselves, we may begin with our far-away neighbors in the 10/40 Window and then come a bit closer to our neighbors in our city, town and neighborhood, but we must include our nearest neighbors—our brothers and sisters in Christ. That's what the next three chapters of Ephesians are all about. Once you have seen your brothers and sisters as the Bride of Christ in the way Paul describes her—as a poem, a tapestry, a cathedral—the only sane way to behave is the way he describes in chapters 4 through 6. In them, the Holy Spirit teaches us what it means to love our nearest neighbors—those right within the Church.

And so in chapter 4 he tells us to preserve the unity of the Spirit through humility and meekness and patience (see 4:2-3), to recognize the diversity of gifts and learn to appreciate one another for our differences (see 4:11-12), to move one another toward maturity (see 4:13) and to speak the truth in love and work together toward the common mission of the Church (see 4:15-16). He tells us to speak the truth to one another (see 4:25), to deal with anger properly (see 4:26), to stop stealing and start working so we can share with others (see 4:28), to speak only those words that are going to build somebody else up, not tear them down (see 4:29), to get rid of bitterness, rage, anger, malice and envy (see 4:31) and to love and forgive one another (see 4:32).

Then in chapter 5 he exhorts us to holiness, with the primary emphasis on harmony in relationships. He tells us to be filled with the Holy Spirit (see 5:18)—and lest we think that's some sort of spine-tingling spiritual high, Paul defines it in hard-to-miss language as talking to one another, worshiping with new and old songs and thanking God for one another (see 5:19-20). And to some people's chagrin, Paul says that loving others in the Church also includes the unfashionable and unpopular concept of *submitting* to one another: husbands to wives, wives to husbands, parents and children to each other, workers and masters likewise (see 5:21-6:9). And the more we see each other like Christ sees the Bride, the more we will love and treat each other in this way.

Finally Paul wraps up with what I think is his dominant motivation for writing the letter in the first place:

> For our struggle is not against flesh and blood, but against the rulers, against the authorities, against the powers of this dark world and against the spiritual forces of evil in the heavenly realms. Therefore put on the full armor of God, so that when the day of evil comes, you may be able to stand your ground, and after you have done everything, to stand. (6:12-13)

Paul has been hinting at this climax all the way through Ephesians. In chapter 1 he says that we have been blessed with spiritual blessing in the heavenly realms and that Christ has been raised to the heavenly realms, above all principalities and powers (see 1:20-21). In chapter 2 he says that we are seated with Christ in the heavenly realms (see 2:6), implying that we are above the principalities and powers. In chapter 3 he says that through the Church, the manifold wisdom of God will be made known to the principalities and powers (see 3:10, KJV). And then in chapter 4, when he says, "Do not let the sun go down while you are still angry" (4:26), even there he gives a cosmic reason for it: "Do not give the devil a foothold" (4:27). And in chapter 6, the gloves are off—he tells us that this is the very reason he's writing the letter. Why do we need to know what the Church is like? So that we can love one another. Why do we need to love one another? So that we can stop fighting each other and start fighting our common enemy.

Satan can't get at the Lord Jesus Christ anymore, so he attacks the Church. He is insanely jealous of the Church. Do you know why? Because the Church is seated with Christ in the heavenly realms, and that's where he wanted to be. He wanted to be enthroned, but God has enthroned Christ and His Church. With this in mind, can you see how ridiculous it is for us to help Satan in his cause by fighting with one another in the Church? That's why one of the most important weapons in the armor of God in chapter 6 is "your feet shod with the preparation of the gospel of peace" (6:15, KJV). It seems that the Roman soldier wore leather shoes with steel-studded soles that gripped the ground because the last thing he wanted, when locked in hand-to-hand combat, was to have his feet give way under him. When we live at peace with one another, it makes us surefooted in the time of battle. So instead of wasting our energies in disharmonious human relationships all the time, let's harness those energies and attack the enemy together.

How do we fight? Paul has given us clues at the beginning and the end of Ephesians. Early in the letter he reminds this church that he is praying for them (see 1:16-17) and specifically prays that they may have the second touch: "I pray also that the eyes of your heart may be enlightened in order that you may know the hope to which he has called you" (1:18). And at the end of the letter, he asks them to pray for one another and to pray for him (see 6:18-20). We fight this battle first of all by praying for one another that the eyes of our hearts will be enlightened so that we will see each other the way that Christ sees us collectively. Then we can launch the weapons of our warfare against the enemy. Warfare is also on Paul's mind when he asks for prayer for himself, because he was preaching the gospel to those who had not yet heard—and that's where the fight is always the severest.

Paul has brought us full circle. When we talked about loving our farthest-away neighbors—those not yet in the kingdom—we concluded that we could best express that love by praying for them. Now Paul tells us that we've got to see the Church the way Christ sees her, and love the Church as He does, in order to fight the battle effectively. And how do we fight that battle? Again, by praying for one another.

The Local Church

With that, Paul is finished—but I'm not. I've got to address a problem that didn't really exist in Paul's day but that is very prevalent in our ruggedly individualistic society. We can listen to a message like this and say, "Yes, I realize that it is wrong to think only of myself as an individual Christian. I need to love the Church of Jesus Christ because I'm part of that Bride." But as we are saying that, we are actually thinking something slightly different. We're thinking, *Sure I love the Church; I'm part of the Church universal. But don't bother me with the local church.* We think of the local church as an artificial distinction that simply does not exist in the Scriptures.

Really? Look at Ephesians 1:1: "Paul, an apostle of Christ Jesus by the will of God, To the saints in Ephesus, the faithful in Christ Jesus." Paul didn't write this letter to the Church universal—he wrote it to an actual, concrete, *local* church (or churches) in Ephesus. (Even if it was written to more than one church, the letter would have been circulated and read in individual *local* churches.)

The universal Church is an abstraction; we cannot love the universal Church. Look at all the injunctions to love in chapters 4 through 6. How can you be humble and meek and submissive to the *universal* Church? You can only do that to the person sitting next to you in the pew or to a member of the board on which you serve together or to the small group of which you are a part. That's where you learn humility and meekness and gentleness. How can you learn to forgive and deal with your anger properly in relation to the universal Church? Eugene Peterson rightly says that "abstraction is the devil's work." Satan doesn't mind if we "love" the universal Church, as long as we don't love those in our own local fellowship. That's all he cares about.

Charles Colson devoted an entire book to the importance of the local church. *The Body* is probably the most important work to come out on this subject in a long, long time. One of the book's most brilliant observations begins with a quote from Calvin on the local church:

> So highly does the Lord esteem the communion of His Church that He considers everyone traitor and apostate from religion who perversely withdraws himself from any Christian society which preserves the true ministry of the word and sacraments.[2]

Calvin's statement may seem a bit harsh, but Colson declares that if God has ordained the Church as the vehicle through which He will spread His gospel and disciple believers, "then one cannot claim to be a Christian and at the same time claim to be outside the church."[3] We are fooling ourselves if we think we can grow as Christians apart from the community of other believers.

The most common objection to this, of course, is that no local church is perfect. This is certainly true. I don't agree *totally* with *all* aspects of *any* particular local church. I think the most illuminating comment on that attitude comes from the pen of Eugene Peterson: "Churches are not Victorian parlors where everything is always picked up and ready for guests. They are messy family rooms."

The early Church, of course, did not have a formal membership policy like many churches—including the one I serve—do today. But they did have an absolutely critical ordinance that essentially accomplished the same purpose (whether or not its primary significance was elsewhere): baptism. Through baptism the individual basically declared to the watching world, "I have broken with my old way of life. I am now united to the Lord Jesus Christ, which makes me a member of the universal Church. But I am also identifying with and making myself accountable to this local, visible community." That usually meant persecution. Outsiders didn't persecute the "universal Church"; they persecuted its local manifestations.

So here are some questions to ponder:

1. *Have you made it unmistakably clear*—by baptism, membership or whatever form is appropriate in your specific situation—*that you have cast your lot with the people of your local church*, which is the particular local representation of the Bride of Christ? If the people of your local church begin to be persecuted, are you likely to be persecuted along with them? Or would the persecuted even know that you are part of the group?

2. *If you were to leave this church, would anyone miss you?* I'm not talking about people who are so busy that they have no time for anybody else. I'm talking about someone, anyone, who would miss you because you've built something into his life and he is sad to see you go. Now turn the question the other way around:

3. *If you were to leave this church, would you miss anyone?* Would it feel like you are wrenching yourself away from a body to which you have been organically united, or would you say, as someone once said to me after leaving her church of thirteen years, "It's no big deal"?

"Just a minute," you might say, "I come faithfully every Sunday morning; I put money in the offering; I sing all the hymns; I listen to the sermon." That isn't good enough! Why not? Consider one final question:

4. *What would you say about someone who slept in your home every night and showed up in time for meals but never helped out—yet he still expected the bed to be made up with fresh linen and the meals all cooked and ready?* What if he never said thank you, never even talked to you unless the meal wasn't done properly? Would you really consider that person a member of your family or not?

These are questions I must ask—questions that only you can answer, and you must do so in light of how Christ sees His Bride. It was said of Winston Churchill that he mobilized the English language and sent it out to battle. This incredible orator pressed his command of the English language into service to fire up the imagination of a whole country to resist the implacable evil of Hitler. That's what the Apostle Paul did in Ephesians. He mobilized the Greek language and sent it into battle, to capture our imaginations with Jesus' view of the Church so that we can learn to love the local church and then get out there and fight the real battle.

Notes

1. Lloyd C. Douglas, *The Robe* (Boston: Houghton Mifflin, 1942), passim.
2. John Calvin, *Institutes of the Christian Religion*, ed. J.T. McNeil, 2 vols. (Philadelphia: Westminster Press, 1960), 2:1012, as quoted by Charles Colson, *The Body* (Dallas: Word, 1992), p. 70.
3. Colson, pp. 70-1.

13. The Quandary of Self-Esteem

In the year 1909, a time when immigration from Europe into the United States was reaching its peak, two immigrants were leaning across the rail of a ship as it passed the Statue of Liberty and slowly made its way into New York harbor. The older one was a fifty-three-year-old Jew who was born in Moravia. Standing next to him was a younger man, a Swiss psychologist. And the older poked the younger in the ribs and said, "Won't they get a surprise when they hear what we have to tell them?" The older man was Sigmund Freud; the younger was Carl Gustav Jung—two of the greatest names in psychology. And what they had to say not only surprised the people of America; it resulted within the next few years in what is today being hailed as the "triumph of the therapeutic."[1]

And it is indeed a triumph. America has six percent of the world's population but thirty-three percent of its psychiatrists and over fifty percent of its clinical psychologists. I am told that New York City alone boasts of more psychologists than all of Europe. And in the year 1989, there were over a hundred more Ph.D.s issued in psychology than in all the rest of the social sciences put together. It is indeed an incredible triumph. One of the most common expressions of this triumph of the therapeutic is the incredibly pervasive importance that has been given to the concept of self-esteem. *Newsweek* magazine labeled this "psycho-theology" and said,

"Of course, you know that there is no such thing as bad people anymore, only people who think badly about themselves."[2]

No sphere of human activity has been left untouched by this triumph of the therapeutic and the pervasiveness of the importance of self-esteem, including theology. *Newsweek* also made the following observation in a 1990 article about the resurgence of religion among baby boomers:

> Unlike earlier religious revivals, the aim this time (apart from born-again traditionalists of all faiths) is support, not salvation, help rather than holiness, a circle of spiritual equals rather than an authoritative church or guide. A group affirmation of self is at the top of the agenda which is why some of the least demanding churches are now in the greatest demand.[3]

"Well, that lets us off the hook," you may say. "Look at the qualifier: 'apart from born-again traditionalists.' " Yes, but that was 1990. Within a few years, the language of self-esteem had become prevalent in evangelical Christian circles—and worse yet, in a way that reflected knee-jerk reaction more than careful thought. Os Guinness, in his book *No God But God*, makes a sobering comment about this disturbing tendency of evangelical Christians to jump on the bandwagon—usually after the band has left town:

> There is a perverse feature of Christian cultural surrender. When Christians freely capitulate to some cultural trend or other, our commitment is often as fierce as it is late. Often it can only be pried loose when the secular world leads Christians to abandon what it earlier led them to adopt. This cycle is already evident in the recovery movement [i.e., twelve-step programs, group therapy, etc.]. The euphoria of latter-day evangelical converts is rising just as secular enthusiasm is waning. *Christianity Today* has many advertisements for recovery

hotlines just when secular books like *The Freudian Fraud* are being published and *Newsweek* has a cover story on the curse of self-esteem. Our motto seems to be, "Buy late, and always be out of date."[4]

Why am I talking about all this, anyway? What does it have to do with loving your neighbor as yourself? Because one area in which self-esteem's pervasiveness has encroached into our lives is the way that this particular commandment—love your neighbor as yourself—has been reinterpreted, even distorted.

This is, by the way, a commandment with a long history of distortion. It was not new with Jesus; way back in Leviticus we were told, "Love your neighbor as yourself" (19:18), but by the time of Jesus, the Pharisees had distorted it into "Love your neighbor and hate your enemy" (Matthew 5:43). So they determined who their neighbor was and wasn't by conveniently excluding everyone they didn't like from the definition of "neighbor." Then there was the expert in the law whom we met in an earlier chapter, who didn't want to exclude or include anybody; he just wanted to have a nice theological discussion about it.

But the modern-day distortion of the commandment doesn't focus on "neighbor"; the triumph of the therapeutic has shifted the focus to "as yourself." The argument goes something like this: "You can't love your neighbor unless you first love yourself. And to love yourself, of course, means that you have high self-esteem. Therefore, what Jesus is *really* saying is that you must first develop high self-esteem. Then you will really love yourself and be able to love your neighbor."

But is that understanding of the verse justifiable? In a word, no. First of all, it is grammatically impossible to translate the verse that way. The plain meaning is very clear; Jesus simply said, "Love your neighbor as you *already* love yourself." Jesus' words only make sense if we grant that He was assuming that the people whom he was talking to already loved themselves in a way that was so self-evident that it did not need further explanation. He said, "What you are already doing to yourself, do to others as well."

And this is certainly the dominant New Testament mentality, for when the Apostle Paul writes in Ephesians about husbands loving their wives, he says, "After all, no one ever hated his own body, but he feeds and cares for it" (5:29). Once again, Paul is using something that we do naturally in order to exhort us to do something that we don't do naturally. The emphasis is not on learning to love ourselves but on recognizing that we *already* love ourselves and so loving others in the same way.

A few moments of thought should help us see how this applies even to those we today call "dysfunctional" people. What are some things that a dysfunctional, lonely person might desire? Well, he might want to be invited out, to be included in a group. That's no surprise; we all naturally feel the same way. Jesus says to do the same to somebody else; if you find a lonely person, invite him into your group.

What does a discouraged, hospitalized person want? He would love to have someone visit him, talk to him, send him flowers or write him a note. That's natural. So what should you do? Visit someone in the hospital, or write him an encouragement card. What does a discouraged, dysfunctional person want? He wants someone to come alongside him, to help, encourage and support him. So what should a discouraged, dysfunctional person do? He should find someone who's discouraged and do the same thing.

Jesus' commandment applies directly to "functional" and dysfunctional people. Certainly many people who have not received appropriate nurturing, especially in those critical years of early childhood, will find it much harder, if not impossible, to encourage, support and otherwise love people compared to those who grew up in emotionally nurturing homes. But that does not allow us to skirt around the plain meaning of what Jesus is saying. And there is absolutely no way in which we can read popular self-esteem "theology" into Jesus' command to love our neighbor as ourselves.

Here's another question I wrestle with: If self-esteem is indeed crucially important to understanding Jesus' command, what do we do with the fact that He gave this command 1,900 years before Freud and Jung landed in North America? Did He give a command that couldn't be understood, let alone obeyed, for 1,900 years? When you pose the question that way, the answer, of course, is no. But that only sets up another question: Does that mean that the modern concern about self-esteem (perhaps self-acceptance is a more appropriate phrase) has no legitimacy at all?

Even a cursory look at some people's lives forces us to acknowledge that there is a very legitimate need to help people gain what one friend of mine calls personal strength. And so the quandary before us is this: If we start from the plain meaning of Jesus' words, there's no way we can pour self-esteem psychology into them. Jesus presupposes that His audience loves themselves in a straightforward way that doesn't have to be learned or brought to them through therapy. But if we start from the undeniable experience of human beings, we have to acknowledge the fact that some people's past experiences, particularly in their early childhoods, have rendered it difficult, if not almost impossible, for them to communicate love to other people.

How do we reconcile this apparent contradiction? In attempting to unravel this problem, I came across the work of Martin Seligman, a secular psychologist considered by some to be the world's leading expert on depression. He found that depression has been on the rise meteorically since World War II in North American society. At the same time, he was puzzled by the findings of a friend of his, a psychological anthropologist. In studying a stone-aged tribe in New Guinea, he could not find anything equivalent to the phenomenon of depression in our society. As he wrestled with this, he identified two dominant characteristics of North American society that have aided this process: the maximizing of self and the minimizing of community.

The maximizing of self occurs because wealth makes it possible for us to have many things, while technology and industry have multiplied our choices. As a result, personal choice becomes increasingly emphasized in this society. With the advertising industry constantly encouraging us to buy and make choices, exercising our choice is also emphasized. These cultural pressures produce what Seligman calls the "maximal self"—the self that sees itself as something that makes decisions on its own.

The minimizing of community, on the other hand, is the result of a gradual eroding of commitment to national and social institutions, according to Seligman. As people turn from national and social commitments, they look inward for meaning and identity. With the breakdown of the nuclear family, a decline in devotion to God and decreasing loyalty to religious institutions, the focus is more and more on the self.

In a situation like this, what happens when we fail? To use Seligman's powerful metaphor, we have no psychological furniture on which to sit down and recover from our failures. The maximized self says, "It's your own fault. You've only got yourself to blame." And the breakdown of community leaves you without help. Helplessness hardens into hopelessness, which is one step away from depression and despair.[5]

Seligman and other experts contend that this rise of individualism and disintegration of community is historically unprecedented and produces a culture of extreme isolation and alienation. This explains why emotional disorders in today's society are of epidemic proportions.

Seligman's insights have helped answer the question that I have struggled with for a long time: Why do we need all this psychologizing to understand a simple commandment of Jesus? Why didn't we need it for the first 1,900 years of Christendom? Isn't it just a problem of sin?

Yes, sin is the problem, but North American society, in maximizing the self and minimizing community, has created new ways for that sin to find expression in our lives. I recall hearing once that Martin Luther defined sin as the "soul curved in upon itself." Over the last several decades, sin has found new ways to curve the soul in upon itself. Some forms of counseling, psychology, therapy, etc. have a very real, necessary and appropriate function in exposing these new machinations of evil within our society.

My understanding of this was amplified by an extract from an essay by David Benner, a Christian psychologist. He begins by saying, "Until one *has* a self, it is difficult to *transcend* self.[6] There's good biblical precedent for this. You may recall that when Jesus washed the feet of His disciples, it was an act of love. The Scripture prefaces the story with these words: "Having loved his own who were in the world, he now showed them the full extent of his love" (John 13:1). What you may not have noticed before is the mind-set of Jesus that made Him act this way:

> Jesus knew that the Father had put all things under his power, and that he had come from God and was returning to God; so he got up from the meal . . . and began to wash his disciples' feet. . . . "You call me 'Teacher' and 'Lord,' and rightly so, for that is what I am." (13:3-5, 13)

Jesus knew four things: who He was, where He had come from, where He was going and what He came to do. Jesus' external act of loving His disciples was rooted very clearly in an accurate self-perception that gave Him a firm grasp on His identity, His destiny and His mission. It is not stretching the point at all to link these two things, to say that how we perceive ourselves in certain critical areas does have a bearing on whether or not we can express love to our neighbor.

Some people, because of their pasts, quite often their childhoods, have indeed had their self-perception—their identities,

missions and destinies—so distorted that it becomes very difficult, if not impossible, for them to serve and love other people.
There's a very legitimate need to help people like that to rees-
tablish their identities and missions, to help them see themselves the way that God sees them in Christ.

Benner's second statement is significant too:

> [Those who] are preoccupied with defending a false self
> . . . have trouble transcending self. . . . In other words,
> they cannot transcend self until they move past the vari-
> ous false selves that are their preoccupations and block
> them from real life. Then, coming to see their true selves
> they are able to understand their need for surrender to
> God.[7]

What does he mean by true self and false self?

People with a distorted self-perception often express it in
self-protective or self-promoting ways. Paul Tournier, the
Swiss psychologist and medical doctor, calls these "weak and
strong reactions." The weak reaction of self-protection produces self-disparagement, excessive submission, self-sacrifice,
underachievement, an "I'm no good" mentality. The strong reaction of self-promotion produces aggression and thrusting
oneself forward, often disguised as strength.

This so-called "high self-esteem" is really nothing but low
self-esteem disguised. For example, it has long been noted
that a large percentage of fanatic military dictators—Hitler,
Stalin, Julius Caesar, Napoleon—were small men trying to
prove that they were big. Their high self-esteem was nothing
more than low self-esteem disguised as self-promotion.

The same point was made in a different way by a very significant study conducted in 1989. Students from eight countries were tested in their mathematical abilities. The lowest
scorers were Americans; the highest scorers were Koreans.
But the same test also measured the students' perception of
their mathematical skills. Guess who rated the highest? The

Americans! And the Koreans rated the lowest. The students who perceived themselves as very good in mathematics were the worst, and those who perceived themselves as being the worst actually did the best. That shows that neither high nor low self-esteem has any direct relation to performance. Perhaps the high self-esteem of the Americans only made them blind to their faults; perhaps the low self-esteem of the Koreans forced them to achieve in order to seek meaning in their lives.

There's another, more obvious danger of high self-esteem: It feeds directly into the fundamental human sin of pride and self-exaltation. A.W. Tozer summed it up very beautifully:

> Self-derogation is bad for the reason that self must be there to derogate. Self, whether swaggering or groveling, can never be anything but hateful to God.
>
> Boasting is an evidence that we are pleased with self; belittling, that we are disappointed in it. Either way we reveal that we have a high opinion of ourselves.[8]

John Piper makes an equally powerful observation about pride disguised as self-pity (another form of self-derogation):

> Both are manifestations of pride. Boasting is the response of pride to success. Self-pity is the response of pride to suffering. Boasting says, "I deserve admiration because I have achieved so much." Self-pity says, "I deserve admiration because I have sacrificed so much." Boasting sounds self-sufficient. Self-pity sounds self-sacrificing. The reason self pity does not look like pride is that it appears to be needy. But the need arises from a wounded ego: the desire of the self-pitying is not really for others to see them as helpless but heroes. The need self pity feels does not come from a sense of unworthiness, but from a sense of unrecognized worthiness. It is the response of unapplauded pride.[9]

To summarize, then: The legitimate role of counseling is to help us deal with emotional traumas from our pasts, especially during childhood; to discern any self-promoting or self-protecting reactions that are really expressions of the sinful soul curved in upon itself; to build a self-awareness and -acceptance, an identity that sees ourselves the way that Christ sees us and thus lifts our eyes off of the false self and yields that true self to God in service to Him.

But even properly understood and applied, therapy and counseling are not enough. There is one other absolutely critical ingredient, agreed upon by Christian and non-Christian psychologists, by theologians and philosophers.

This one critical element in learning to discover who we are so that we can yield our true selves to God and love our neighbor as ourselves is community. If Seligman was right and the minimizing of community was a critical contributor to the problem, rediscovery of community, especially Christian community, is absolutely essential to its solution. Benner puts it this way:

> To attempt to find self apart from others is to fail to find our true self. True selfhood is a gift we receive from others; in relationship to others we find who we truly are. Developing meaningful attachments to others is, therefore, a necessary step in the discovery of identity and the achievement of psychological maturity.[10]

What sorts of things should community provide that will enable this discovery of our true selves so that we can transcend those selves and serve God and others?

The first critical component that community provides is a safe place for confession. James says, "Confess your sins to each other and pray for each other so that you may be healed" (5:16). Relational honesty, openness, vulnerability: These are absolutely essential to discovering ourselves.

Those who did not experience, at least to a reasonable extent, this kind of community (usually when they were growing up), may, to varying degrees, have their souls curved in upon themselves in twisted, self-preoccupying ways. The refusal to make ourselves vulnerable to a community of people may be one of the greatest obstacles to truly discovering ourselves.

Those of us who are fortunate enough, by the grace of God, to have had healthy childhoods and are emotionally mature and whole have a tendency to dismiss all of this with statements like, "Self-image is just psychobabble," whether we articulate them or not. Maybe our job ought to be to start providing genuine community for those who need it—a listening ear; a safe environment where people can confess; a place where they can become vulnerable, honest and open for the first time. If we did that, maybe the therapist's couch and the bartender's ear, which really serve the same purpose, would not be as necessary.

But James goes on to say, "And pray for each other so that you may be healed" (5:16). That's the second critical element in discovering self.

It is easy to say, "Yes, we must restore our identity, mission and destiny." It is easy to say, "We must see ourselves the way Christ sees us." But nothing is harder than getting people to see themselves that way. The eighteen inches that separates head from heart is in many ways the longest journey that anyone can undertake. And while therapy and listening ears may help in this journey, the one thing that is indispensable to taking truth acknowledged in the mind and engraving it upon sinful human hearts is the ministry of the Holy Spirit. This, in turn, means that prayer—caring, loving, focused prayer in the community—is an absolutely critical element.

Leanne Payne[11], a counselor and psychologist who has led hundreds of people into maturity and wholeness, tells in one of her books the story of a young woman named Enid who had a terrible father. He deserted the family, leaving them destitute with nothing but a tiny little farm on which to scratch out a living. He had even tried to burn down the farmhouse once. Her mother was a poor immigrant woman who hardly spoke English.

Yet Enid and her brother both grew up psychologically whole. She served God faithfully for nearly fifty years in a Christian ministry, and her brother became a faithful pastor. Want to know their secret? Payne says it was simply prayer. Their mother communicated a deep and abiding sense of the Fatherhood of God by the intimacy and faith that she demonstrated in her prayers with them.

One of my most tragic observations has been the reluctance of therapists, even Christian therapists, to pray with the people they are counseling. It reflects the reluctance of so many Christians to pray with one another. We're too busy spouting advice. What if we talked less to them and talked more to God with them? Why this reluctance?

Payne suggests that it could be simple spiritual laziness for most of us. In the case of a therapist, it may be a misguided desire to maintain a "professional distance" with his clients. Whatever the reasons are that keep us from praying, we need to realize that it is a second critical ingredient of community that helps people discover their true selves.

There's a third critical ingredient as well: affirmation and accountability. A loving community can affirm people who are journeying toward emotional wholeness by encouraging and helping them discover their gifts, temperaments and passions so that they can serve God in the way that He has uniquely wired them for significance. Community helps them dream big, then comes alongside and holds their hands when they step out into their divinely appointed destinies for the first time. And then community holds them accountable to continue doing so.

I was amazed at the way Seligman—a secular, non-Christian expert on depression—concluded his article. His advice for dealing with the maximized self is something he calls "moral jogging"—a series of practices intended to increase one's concern for others. They include such things as:

- Put aside five percent of last year's taxable income (*not* "take-home" pay) and give it away personally.

- Give up some activity you do regularly and spend the time instead in an activity devoted to the well-being of somebody else; give one evening a week to do this.

- When asked by a homeless person for money, *talk* to him. Frequent areas where you will find beggars, talk to them and give no less than $5 to those who are truly in need. Spend three hours a week doing this.

- When you read of particularly heroic or despicable acts, write letters of praise or rebuke. Spend three more hours a week doing this.[12]

If a Christian pastor said that to people, he would be accused of manipulation, legalism, insensitivity and so on. Yet this man, considered by the non-Christian academic world to be a leading expert on depression, says that these practices are good for a depressed person.[13] In other words, he has come to the opposite conclusion of those who say that you should learn to love yourself in order to love others. He says that you need to start loving others so that you can love yourself.

The place where we begin to do this is in Christian community: a place that is safe enough for us to become honest and open and vulnerable; a place where people who know God and love us are willing to pray to the heavenly Father that the Holy Spirit will impress our true identity in Christ on our hearts; a place where people will both affirm us in what God has given to us and hold us accountable to use those gifts in loving one another.

Notes

1. Os Guinness and John Seel, eds., *No God But God: Breaking with the Idols of Our Age* (Chicago: Moody, 1992), p. 111; story taken from Ernest Becker, *The Denial of Death* (New York: Free Press, 1973), p. 96.

2. Jerry Adler, "Hey, I'm Terrific!" *Newsweek*, February 17, 1992, p. 42, as quoted in Guinness and Seel, *No God But God*, p. 127.

3. Kenneth L. Woodward et al., "A Time to Seek," *Newsweek*, December 17, 1990, p. 17.

4. Guinness and Seel, p. 120.

5. Martin E.P. Seligman, *Learned Optimism* (New York: Knopf, 1991), pp. 282-6.

6. David Benner, *Psychotherapy and the Spiritual Quest* (Grand Rapids, MI: Baker, 1988), p. 123.

7. Ibid., pp. 123-4.

8. A.W. Tozer, *Man: The Dwelling Place of God* (Camp Hill, PA: WingSpread Publishers, 1966), p. 71.

9. John Piper, *Future Grace* (Sisters, OR: Multnomah, 1998), pp. 94-5.

10. Benner, p. 128.

11. Leanne Payne has written several good books on prayer and God's power to heal our inner wounds. One of her best is *The Healing Presence* (Grand Rapids, MI: Baker, 1995).

12. Seligman, p. 289.

13. I am fully aware that the problem of depression has only become even more pervasive in our society and in our churches since 1994 when I first read Seligman's observations and preached the sermon from which this chapter was derived. In February 2003 we had Dr. Grant Mullin, another expert on depression, give a two-hour seminar in our church. Nearly 400 people jammed the sanctuary. Over the past eighteen months, I have also been closely associated with two or three people who have courageously faced acute depression. Their recovery was not easy, formulaic or simply achieved by giving money to the poor and otherwise helping those less fortunate. So the problem of depression is ubiquitous and complex. I do not offer Seligman's observations as an easy, "See, I told you so" cure for all sorts of depression. However, his insights are valuable in that they underline certain dimensions of the causes of, and remedies for, depression that I don't hear very often from those in the mental health professions. And they (Seligman's observations) are certainly very much to the point in correcting the misunderstanding of Jesus' commandment as teaching that we can't love others unless we love ourselves. That may well be true, but we can't read that into Jesus' words.

Epilogue: Are You *in* the Kingdom?

We have taken thirteen chapters to explore in depth what might be involved in obeying Jesus' commandments to love God with all our hearts, souls, minds and strength and to love our neighbor as ourselves. We have no way of knowing what went through the mind of the teacher of the law whose question elicited Jesus' declaration. We do know what he said, and I am fascinated by his response:

> "Well said, teacher," the man replied. "You are right in saying that God is one and there is no other but him. To love him with all your heart, with all your understanding and with all your strength, and to love your neighbor as yourself is more important than all burnt offerings and sacrifices." (Mark 12:32-33)

This man realized something that had been lost on most of his contemporaries: that religion involves much more than the performance of ritual—even rituals that God Himself prescribed. He knew and understood that religion has to go beyond ritual to relationship. I am even more fascinated by Jesus' reply to him, because he had responded so wisely: "You are not far from the kingdom of God" (12:34). That was good news for him, because he was moving toward the kingdom. But it also struck me, as I was meditating upon this passage, that when Jesus said, "You are not far from the kingdom," it also meant that he wasn't *in* the kingdom. And that's bad news for some people who think that they are in the kingdom but may only be close.

What is involved in that awful possibility? Can a person be as close to the kingdom as this teacher of the law and still miss the boat? Is there any hope for such a soul? I plan to answer these questions, but first I would like to review what we've learned in this study of these two commandments of Jesus. If I could summarize all that I have wanted to say in this book, it would be that to love God with all of your heart, mind and strength and to love your neighbor as yourself require the making or renewal of three commitments: (1) a commitment to renewing your heart through a life of prayer and worship by the use of Scripture, poetry and music regularly; (2) a commitment to renewing your mind through a life of reading theology, history and literature; and (3) a commitment to renewing relationships in a larger worshiping community and a smaller caring community, where you can practice vulnerability and accountability.

If I were to ask you how the call to these sorts of commitments has affected you, what would you say? Has there been any change in your life? Has there been any movement toward God in any one of these directions? I know, praise God, that many who heard the original sermon series were able to answer positively and recount specific ways that their lives have changed. I am hopeful that your journey through this book has had a similar effect in your life.

But I cannot ignore the possibility that you may have read this far but have not been changed at all. Your heart may be just as unmoved by the possibility of developing intimacy with God through worship, prayer and meditation and your mind just as uninterested in theology, history and literature as you were before you picked up this book. Your priorities—the way you spend your money and your time—may still lie unexamined. You may be no more committed to a local congregation than you ever were before, and you may have not yet made yourself accountable to anybody, whether it be an individual or a small group. You may agree with everything that you have read. "Yes," you say, "it makes total sense. This is how to love God with all your heart, mind and strength, and to love your neighbor as yourself." You agree with it all—just as you agree that a ruler is twelve inches long. But the bottom line is that there has been no movement, no change, no further interest.

If so, I have to ask you to consider what the real issue might be. The question may not be how to get you to be obedient but whether you are really *in* the kingdom at all. Has your heart ever been changed from a hard, stony heart to a heart that can be engraved with the law, the love and the fear of God? Has your mind ever been renewed from a darkened, ignorant mind to one that can be renewed in knowledge and righteousness and holiness? Have you ever been organically united to a body, or is it still a mechanical connection? In short, have you ever been born again by the Spirit of God?

That's a hard question. And you might even respond by saying, "Just a minute. You can't say that to me—I believe!" You can even point to a date, a time, a place when you made a commitment—went to the altar, lifted your hand, signed a card. "Yes," you say, "I believe." But let's take a closer look at what it means to believe. John Piper, in his book *Desiring God*, makes this painful observation:

> We are surrounded by unconverted people who think they do believe in Jesus. Drunks on the street say they believe. Unmarried couples sleeping together say they believe. Elderly people who haven't sought worship or fellowship for forty years say they believe. All kinds of lukewarm, world-loving, church attenders say they believe. The world abounds with millions of unconverted people who say they believe.[1]

The phrase "I believe" is empty. My responsibility as a preacher of the gospel and a teacher in the Church is not to preserve and repeat cherished phrases but to pierce the heart with biblical truth. Let's look at another of Piper's observations about what "I believe" really means. Isaiah 43:6-7 says, "Bring my sons from afar / and my daughters from the ends of the earth— / everyone who is called by my name, / whom I created for my glory." Step number one, Piper says, is to acknowledge that we have one and only one primary purpose for being created, and that is to glorify God. To glorify God, of course, means to value, to acknowledge, to treasure and to take pleasure in His glory—who He is and what His goals are in the world.[2]

Piper is saying that every aspect of life needs to somehow be pervaded by, and eventually linked to, our love for the glory of God. That echoes the apostle Paul's command: "So whether you eat or drink or whatever you do, do it all for the glory of God" (1 Corinthians 10:31).

Of course, this is the exact opposite of what we've done. The Bible says in Romans 3:23, "All have sinned and fall short of the glory of God." What does "sin" mean? It doesn't mean the proverbial little black book in our mental filing cabinet with its lists of dos and don'ts. It means the fundamental choice that we have made of exchanging the glory of the Creator for the glory of created things—whether they happen to be filthy or noble created things is beside the point.

But God, in His great mercy, provided a way for sinful people like you and me to come back to Him, without sacrificing His justice, through Jesus Christ's death on the cross. He offered us eternal life. And how do we receive this eternal life? The first step, of course, is what we all know: We have to believe. Acts 16:31 says, "Believe in the Lord Jesus, and you will be saved." But that's not the whole story. There are several other verses that give us many different slants on what it means to receive eternal life. Acts 3:19 says, "Repent, then, and turn to God, so that your sins may be wiped out." Hebrews 5:9 says that Jesus "became the source of eternal salvation for all who obey him."

And Luke 10:25, the parallel passage to the one we looked at in Mark, says, "On one occasion an expert in the law stood up to test Jesus. 'Teacher,' he asked, 'what must I do to inherit eternal life?' " And you know Jesus' answer by now: "You must love God with all your heart, soul, mind and strength and your neighbor as yourself." So you see, to receive eternal life doesn't mean just to believe; it means the whole package: to believe, to repent, to obey, to love God with all your heart, soul, mind and strength and to love your neighbor as yourself.

What ties all these different aspects of receiving eternal life together in such a way that they don't become another rule? What is the underlying unity behind them? Piper has given the best answer I have seen to date. He focuses on Matthew 13:44: "The kingdom of heaven is like treasure hidden in a field. When a man found it, he hid it again, and then in his joy [or literally, *from* his joy] went and sold all he had and bought that field."

This parable of the kingdom of heaven says that somewhere in the process of receiving eternal life, joy is kindled within our hearts; desire is born. Piper says:

> I conclude from this parable that we must be deeply converted in order to enter the kingdom of heaven, and we are converted when Christ becomes for us a Treasure Chest of holy joy. . . . It implies that beneath and behind the act of faith which pleases God, a new taste has been created. A taste for the glory of God and the beauty of Christ. Behold, a joy has been born! . . . [Until then, God] was an idea—even a good one—and a topic for discussion; but he was not a treasure of delight.
>
> Then something miraculous happened. . . . First the stunned silence before the unspeakable beauty of holiness. Then a shock and terror that we had actually loved the darkness. Then the settling stillness of joy that this is the soul's end. . . .

And then, faith—the confidence that Christ has made
a way for me, a sinner, to live in his glorious fellowship
forever, the confidence that if I come to God through
Christ, he will give me the desire of my heart to share his
holiness and behold his glory.

But before the confidence comes the craving. Before
decision comes delight. Before trust comes the discovery
of treasure. . . . Saving faith is a heartfelt conviction not
only that Christ is reliable, but that he is desirable.[3]

He's saying that any conversion that does not create a new
taste for the glory, greatness, love and beauty of God and
Christ is not genuine.

To drive home the seriousness of this, let me make the
point in a completely different way. Imagine that you meet
someone who confesses to having a lack of desire for God,
and you confront him with the possibility that he is not *in*
the kingdom of God. Suppose that person says, "Hey! I believe! Do you want to know my statement of faith? I am
monotheistic. I believe there is one God. I don't worship
idols. I believe that Jesus Christ is the Son of the Most High
God. I believe that Jesus Christ is going to come back one day
to judge wickedness. I believe in the message of salvation and
in world missions. I believe that the Apostle Paul was a servant of the Most High God, who, in his missionary journeys,
preached the true way of salvation to Gentiles."

How would you respond to someone who says that he be-
lieves all of those things? Most of us would say that person is
not just a Christian but a committed one. And yet every one of
those statements is attributed in the Bible to the demonic
world (see James 2:19 and Acts 16:16ff for two examples).
Someone has astutely observed that there is no such thing as a
liberal demon in hell. Every one of them is an orthodox, Bible-
believing, evangelical demon. They know the truth. What's
missing? It's a love and passion for the holiness of God and the
beauty of Jesus Christ.

Some may think it unkind to suggest to someone who lacks desire for God that he may be outside the kingdom. But if that is his real state, to try to reassure him is the worst thing we can do. It would not be a loving thing at all. Jonathan Edwards put it magnificently in his *Treatise on Religious Affections* (the archaic English may require careful reading, but it is well worth the effort):

> For so hath God contrived and constituted things, in his dispensations towards his own people, that when their love decays . . . fear should arise . . . when love rises, and is in vigorous exercise, then fear should vanish and be driven away. . . . There are no other principles, which human nature is under the influence of, that will ever make men conscientious, but one of these two, *fear* or *love* . . . and therefore God has wisely ordained that these two opposite principles of love and fear should rise and fall, like the two opposite scales of a balance. . . . Love is the spirit of adoption, or the childlike principle; if that slumbers, men fall under fear, which is the spirit of bondage. . . . And if it be so, that love, or the spirit of adoption, be carried to a great height, it drives away all fear, and gives full assurance; agreeable to that of the apostle, 1 John 4:18, "There is no fear in love, but perfect love casts out fear." . . . [That is why] when love is asleep . . . in vain is all the saint's self-examinations, and poring on past experience, in order to establish his peace, and get assurance. For it is contrary to the nature of things, as God hath constituted them, that he should have assurance at such a time.
>
> They therefore do directly thwart God's wise and gracious constitution of things, who exhort others to be confident in their hope, when in dead frames; under a notion of "living by faith, and not by sight, and trusting God in the dark, and living upon Christ, and not upon experiences"; and who warn them not to doubt of their good estate, lest they should be guilty of the dreadful sin of unbelief. And it has a direct tendency to establish the most presumptuous hypocrites, and to prevent their ever

calling their state into question. . . . And doubtless vast has
been the mischief that has been done this way.[4]

There is a very fine line between comforting the afflicted
with the promises of God and afflicting the comfortable with
the warnings of God. In fact, the line is so fine that only the
Holy Spirit can do it. And one of the ways in which He does
it is remarkable—the same passages that make those who are
not yet truly in the kingdom anxious for their souls, when
spoken into the heart of those who *are* in the kingdom, stir
up within their hearts new desires to seek after God with all
their hearts, souls, minds and strength.

And so, if you have read this book and have not changed,
and you have no real desire to change, I can't let you hide behind a simplistic "I believe" theology. Are you really born
again in the Spirit of God or not? Are you merely not too far
from the kingdom but not in it? If questions like that make
you anxious for the welfare of your soul, well, that was my
whole intention!

The customary practice in many churches where people
who come to the altar are given a few bromides to quickly
settle their spiritual anxiety is a recent phenomenon that was
largely unknown for the first nineteen centuries of the
Church. During the great evangelical awakenings of the eighteenth and nineteenth centuries, when people came forward
in response to the preaching of Whitefield, Edwards, Moody,
Torrey and others, I understand that the front row was called
the "anxious seat"—for people who had become anxious
about the condition of their souls. They were not given
quick, palliative answers and told to pray the sinner's prayer
to "accept Christ" (a phrase that A.W. Tozer often pointed
out is not found anywhere in the Bible); they were told to go
home and continue to be anxious, to cry out for God to have
mercy upon them. They were not just asking God to give
them a passport to heaven. During these times of revival

awakenings, the initial impact of the Spirit upon repentant souls was a deep conviction of sin by which they *felt* their just dessert was to be banished to hell. Then when they broke through to a sense of Christ's love and grace, their love for Him was all the greater and deeper.

If you think there is any chance that you might be not far from, but not in, the kingdom, I would encourage you to reread this book—not because I wrote it, but because Jesus Christ said that these commandments are the two most important things. Read it in a private place where you can stop in the middle if you have to and cry out to God to have mercy upon you. Keep reading through all the chapters until the Word of God has begun to grip your heart and you sense the beginnings of a passion for the glory of God and the beauty of Christ. Whatever you do, don't remain in your condition of disinterest. Don't let the next six months be like the last six months or the six months before that, because then your heart is slowly being hardened. The longer you wait, the harder it will be to come back.

But if, on the other hand, you are born again, you do have a desire for God and you have made steps forward—small or big—to grow in your love for Him and for your neighbor, I praise God for that! You might want to reread this book as well, but for a totally different reason—not to awaken thirst but to continue to move you forward, to act as a motivator, to keep driving you to that spring of Living Water so that you can move from strength to strength as you love God with all your heart, soul, mind and strength.

As I was making a final review of this material, my mind went back to what at first seemed like a totally unrelated memory. I began to think of a game I played as a child called "Chutes and Ladders." The game board consists of a series of ladders with numbered rungs; you roll the dice on each turn to see how many rungs you can climb, and the object of the game is to eventually reach the top—100. There are chutes at some of the rungs, however, and if you land on one of those, you slide down to a lower rung. The chute that everyone really dreads is at rung #98—just two rungs before the top. The goal is to get past #98, because if you land on it, that chute slides you all the way down to the first rung! I always laughed when that happened—I got so close to the top, and then I had to start all over again!

That was funny, but I saw the serious side to it when I read John Bunyan's *Pilgrim's Progress*. In that allegory of the Christian life, the hero saw a road to hell right at the entrance to heaven. It's possible to be so near the kingdom and yet be really, really far.

If you need to begin that process of crying out to God right now, by all means do so. If you simply want to reaffirm to the Lord that you are more determined than ever to love God with all your heart, soul, mind and strength, take time to do that as well. Just don't be like Jacob, who, after hearing from God in a dream, awoke and said, "Surely the LORD is in this place, and I was not aware of it" (Genesis 28:16).

Notes

1. John Piper, *Desiring God* (Sisters, OR: Multnomah, 1986), p. 54.
2. Ibid., p. 55.
3. Ibid., pp. 66-9.
4. Jonathan Edwards, *Treatise on Religious Affections* (public domain e-text published by InspirationalMedia.com), n.d., p. 61. Available from: <http://www.inspirational media.com/affections.pdf>.

A
STUDY GUIDE

for

LOVING GOD
WITH ALL YOU'VE GOT

BY DONALD P. SMITH

STUDY GUIDE

Some people can skim through a book and retain virtually every thought that they read. However, most of us don't own a thought until we mentally massage it several times. That's one reason that we often find "new" insights when we reread a thought-full book. This study guide is dedicated to helping the reader visit again some of the insights in *Loving God with All You've Got*. It makes no attempt to outline or review every point that the book makes but simply provides a track through which to mentally massage some of the material found in the book so that the reader can "own" more of it.

The initial idea for developing a study guide for *Loving God . . .* came out of the use of this book as curriculum for a study group. While this guide is an extension of the notes from that teaching situation, an individual who is studying alone should also be able to benefit from it by simply adapting the questions to individual study. Where the guide calls for discussion, translate it as "meditation."

If you are using *Loving God . . .* as curriculum for a group, you will find that the group's dynamics will give your study a character of its own. Our group averaged fifteen mature adults. After opening prayer for the concerns of the group, we had forty-five to fifty minutes for study and closing prayer. Sometimes we were not able to complete a chapter in one session because of the length of our discussion and the leader's unwillingness to cut short that meaningful involvement. I'd recommend that you forget the schedule and let the discussions roll.

It is my hope that you (and your study group) will find this book and study guide helpful in developing new levels of relationship with our personal and transcendent God.

—Rev. Donald P. Smith

Chapter 1: The Anatomy of Idolatry

Key Thought: Idolatry is alive and thriving because "the ultimate idol factory is the human heart."[1]

1. What does it mean to love God with all your heart? Why is *heart* a significant Bible term?
2. Why does God get so upset about idolatry?
3. The author states that we commit idolatry by "miniaturizing" and "vaporizing" God. Explain this. Is this true in your life?
4. Read Jeremiah 23. Is there a relationship between the teachings of the false prophets of Jeremiah's day and our cry of "God bless America"?
5. Discuss what the author means when he states, "You cannot split the transcendence of God from the immanence of God." (For further consideration of this thought, see *The Attributes of God*, volume 2, chapter 2, by A.W. Tozer.)
6. In what ways does the worship of the one true God differ from the worship of "near and faraway" idols?

Chapter 2: Loving God's Word

Key Thought: We bring the "faraway" God near by learning to love His Word.

1. Read Jeremiah 31:33 and Romans 5:5. Are these two verses incongruous? Why or why not, according to the author?
2. How does the attitude to the law of the Lord found in the book of Psalms differ from our customary negative reaction to God's law? (See Psalms 1:2; 19:7-11; 119:97, 105, 111; 147:19-20.)
3. In what ways does God's law order the "inner space" within our lives? (See Psalm 119:9-11, 32, 45-46, 98-100, 165.) Have you experienced this in your own life?

4. How is it that we can both *fear* the law and *love* it at the same time? (See Psalm 119:61, 63.)

5. What words from Scripture (e.g., *death, sin, freedom, hell, joy, salvation,* etc.) have lost their meaning in our churches and culture today? Why do you think this is so? What solutions does the author suggest?

6. Read Psalm 119:65-72. Visualize the affliction of the psalmist; then consider the psalmist's new awakening through renewing his relationship with God.

7. As the author recommends, take time this week to read Psalm 119 each day. Then reflect upon what God is saying to you about His law.

Chapter 3: Worship

Key Thought: "The most appropriate response of the creature to the Creator is that of ascribing worth, or worship."

(Note: *Worship* is the reverent love and allegiance accorded a deity, idol or sacred object; a set of ceremonies, prayers or other religious forms by which that love is expressed; ardent, humble devotion. *Worship* comes from Old English: *weorth* + *scipe* = worth-ship or worthy to receive honor.[2])

1. What are some Old and New Testament evidences that men and women were created for the purpose of worshiping God, the Creator?

2. How will Christ's work of redemption one day restore us to our original function as worshipers of God?

3. What are some of the "feelings" associated with worship?

4. Discuss the difference between the words *eros* and *agape*. Why does the author say that only *eros* is appropriate when it comes to loving God?

5. Read Ephesians 5:19 and Colossians 3:16. Then discuss the role of psalms, hymns and choruses in our personal and corporate worship times.

6. Additional thoughts for further reflection and discussion:

   a. "When God commands us to sing, it is not a test of our ability—it is a test of our love."

   b. "An open Bible and an open hymnal are two of the most powerful tools . . . to learn to love God with all of my heart and to love His law."

Chapter 4: Forgotten Fundamentals of an Integrated Life

Key Thought: "God has done what only God can do to give us unified, undivided hearts out of which will flow integrated lives."

1. What are the three underlying fundamentals of an integrated Christian life?

2. If Jesus were to reorder your priorities, how differently might you spend your time? Your money? Your energy?

3. What is the responsibility of the Christian to continue discipleship training?

4. Who was/is the most influential mentor in your life? Do you offer yourself to others as a mentor? (For further study of mentoring, see *The Power of Mentoring: Shaping People Who Will Shape the World* by Martin Sanders.)

5. Have you received a specific calling? Are you exercising your spiritual gift(s) through ministry in your local church?

6. How can you bring the discipline of an integrated life into your secular vocation? Is this a new thought for you? If so, what bearing might it have upon your current attitude toward your work?

Chapter 5: A Theology of the Mind

Key Thought: "It is impossible to love God and not be a theologian."[3]

1. According to Scripture, what are the characteristics of the human mind in its natural state? (See Romans 1:21; 2 Corinthians 4:4; Ephesians 4:17-18.)
2. In what ways is Satan using today's culture to attack our minds? What are intentional methods you have used to thwart Satan's efforts?
3. What is a "divided mind," and what are its symptoms? (See Colossians 2:18-19; 1 Timothy 6:3-5; James 4:8.)
4. Read First Corinthians 14:20. In what ways are we to be adults in our thinking?
5. What are some common objections to becoming a "theologian"? How does the author answer these objections?
6. What is the urgency for fostering an integrated mind? (See Philippians 3:13-15; 1 Peter 1:13; 4:7; Revelation 17:9.)

Chapter 6: Confronting Modernity

Key Thought: "If we want to change the culture in which we live . . . we need to . . . understand the culture and stop it from influencing us."

1. Discuss the author's concept of modernity. How has modernity become so prevalent?
2. Who are the "gatekeepers" in our society? Who "controls" our society's thoughts?
3. How have "secularization," "pluralization" and "privatization" contributed to the rapid separation of church and state?
4. What influence has pluralism (e.g., the acceptance of the homosexual lifestyle; the acceptance of Mormons, Mus-

lims and all "faith groups" as valid forms of worship) had in your community? Does this differ from ancient Israel's decline into idolatry?

5. What are some other doctrinal teachings (e.g., salvation is through faith in Jesus Christ alone) that are in jeopardy of being watered down by the "4As" (i.e., assumption, abandonment, adaptation, assimilation)?

6. What are some concrete steps you will take this week to take "every thought captive" to make it obedient to Jesus Christ?

Chapter 7: Remembering the Past

Key Thought: "History is the greatest antidote to the disease of modernity."

1. Can you think of some "subtle art forms" in today's culture that subvert the truth of the gospel?

2. How does the media treat God as a factor in the history of the United States? How does the educational community teach faith as a part of history? (Examples: the faith of George Washington, Abraham Lincoln or Dwight D. Eisenhower.)[4]

3. The author suggests several ways that remembering history can enrich our lives and embolden our faith. How have you personally been encouraged and informed by the past?

4. Which Christian book, other than the Bible, has impacted you the most? Share this with your group.

Chapter 8: Objections, Obstacles, Costs

Key Thought: Loving God with all our minds involves the intentional discipline of regular reading.

1. Name some of the legitimate and not-so-legitimate reasons why people do not read more than they do.
2. Discuss ways that we can be obedient to these scriptural exhortations: "Prepare your minds for action. . . . Always be prepared to give . . . the reason for the hope that you have" (1 Peter 1:13; 3:15).
3. Discuss the books that have been meaningful to you and your family members.
4. Develop a short list of books that you and your group will commit to read and discuss over the next year.
5. Choose a particular book and agree as a group to read it and journal after each chapter. Then come to group meetings prepared to share your various journal entries.

Chapter 9: With All Your Strength

Key thought: We have the incredible privilege of drawing near to the most holy God through Jesus Christ.

1. After rereading the story of King Josiah (see 2 Kings 22-23:25), attempt to "visualize, personalize and vocalize" (see chapter 2) this story in an effort to relive the passion of Josiah.
2. The author cites five biblical warnings against forsaking God (see Hebrews 2:1-3; 3:12; 6:4-6; 10:26-27; 12:25). What is the relevance of these five warnings to loving God with all our hearts, souls, minds and strength?
3. The author describes a "*kairos* moment" as a unique opportunity in time to act; it is unique in that if you miss the opportunity, it may never come again. Have you ever had such a moment in your life? What stops us from taking hold of the *kairos* moments of our lives?

4. Ephesians 6 makes it clear that believers are engaged in a spiritual battle. Do you feel this tension in your own life? What have been your victories? Your defeats?

5. Consider how you would respond to this statement: "God wants you to drive home a stake of commitment to love God with all you've got. Will you do it?"

Chapter 10: Loving the Lost

Key Thought: Every believer is commissioned to love his distant ("unreached") neighbors "for His Name's sake."

1. Can we love God and not be interested in *His* great interest? Why or why not?

2. Though the task to reach the unsaved is seemingly insurmountable, what is the role of faith? (See Mark 10:26-27; John 10:16; Romans 10:17.)

3. What will be some of the "costs" associated with our personal involvement in frontier missions?

4. What keeps us from doing more to love our distant neighbors?

5. What insight does the author give with regard to viewing our involvement in frontier missions as a sacrifice? (See Mark 10:28-30.)

Chapter 11: Your Nearby Neighbor

Key Thought: The near and distant lost are our obligation and our opportunity to strengthen our spiritual gifts.

1. Discuss the definition of "nearby neighbor." What are some of the opportunities for loving the nearby neighbors in your community?

2. Who are the modern-day "lepers" in our society who long for a touch of compassion?

3. Share about an experience or encounter in your life that caused you to become burdened for a person/people in need.

4. Do you know your spiritual gift(s)? How have you been able to use it in your local church? What accountability structures have been put in place?

Chapter 12: Loving the Bride

Key Thought: To love our neighbors as ourselves includes loving our "nearest neighbors," our brothers and sisters in Christ.

1. How has the discussion in this chapter helped you see the individuals in your congregation as God's artwork or poetry?

2. Read and discuss Ephesians 4:1-16.

3. To what extent are you now more aware of the seriousness of the statement that "the Church is the devil's number one target"?

4. Discuss the following quote from Calvin: "So highly does the Lord esteem the communion of His Church that He considers everyone traitor and apostate from religion who perversely withdraws himself from any Christian society."[5]

5. If you were to leave your local church, would anyone miss you? Would you miss anyone?

Chapter 13: The Quandary of Self-Esteem

Key Thought: It is in relationship to others that we discover who we truly are, thus enabling us to serve God and others.

1. The author shows how we have been subjected to the self-esteem psychology that says we must love ourselves

first in order to love others. How does this line up with Jesus' command to love our neighbors as ourselves?

2. What are some ways the author suggests that a Christian community can help you discover your true self?

3. List some practical things you can do (individually and/or as a group) on a small scale to increase your concern for others.

4. As a result of reading through this book, share at least one new idea or thought you have with regard to:

    a. loving God with all your heart;

    b. loving God with all your mind;

    c. loving God with all your strength;

    d. loving your neighbor as yourself.

Notes

1. Os Guinness and John Seel, eds., *No God But God: Breaking with the Idols of Our Age* (Chicago: Moody, 1992), p. 27.

2. From *The American Heritage Dictionary of the English Language, New College Edition* (Boston: Houghton Mifflin, 1981), n.p.

3. Guinness and Seel, p. 19.

4. For more examples, see *America Built on Character, Founded on Faith* by Mark Ammerman (Camp Hill, PA: Christian Publications, Inc., 2004).

5. John Calvin, *Institutes of the Christian Religion*, ed. J.T. McNeil, 2 vols. (Philadelphia: Westminster Press, 1960), 2:1012, as quoted by Charles Colson, *The Body* (Dallas: Word, 1992), p. 70.